Poetry 2

John L. Foster

Nelson

This Series consists of:

Poetry 1, 2 and 3
Story 1, 2 and 3
Drama 1, 2 and 3
Language 1, 2 and 3

Thomas Nelson and Sons Ltd
Nelson House Mayfield Road
Walton-on-Thames Surrey
KT12 5PL UK

51 York Place
Edinburgh
EH1 3JD UK

Thomas Nelson (Hong Kong) Ltd
Toppan Building 10/F
22A Westlands Road
Quarry Bay Hong Kong

Thomas Nelson Australia
102 Dodds Street
South Melbourne
Victoria 3205 Australia

Nelson Canada
1120 Birchmount Road
Scarborough Ontario
M1K 5G4 Canada

© John L Foster 1987

First published by Macmillan Education Ltd 1987
ISBN 0-333-43662-8

This edition published by Thomas Nelson and Sons Ltd 1992

ISBN 0-17-432449-9
NPN 9 8 7 6 5 4 3 2

All rights reserved. No paragraph of this publication may be reproduced, copied or transmitted save with written permission or in accordance with the provisions of the Copyright, Design and Patents Act 1988, or under the terms of any licence permitting limited copying issued by the Copyright Licensing Agency, 90 Tottenham Court Road, London W1P 9HE.

Any person who does any unauthorised act in relation to this publication may be liable to criminal prosecution and civil claims for damages.

Printed in Hong Kong.

Contents

Acknowledgements	iv
1: I Remember...	1
2: Comparison Poems	12
3: Advice and Warning Poems	24
4: Senses Poems	32
5: Conversation Poems	52
6: Advertisement Poems	60
7: Adjective Poems	67
8: Snapshot Poems	74
9: Letter Poems	87
10: Haiku, Tanka, Cinquains and Diamond Poems	97
11: Adverb Poems	104
12: Story Poems	114

Acknowledgements

The author and publishers wish to thank the following who have kindly given permission for the use of copyright material;

Associated Book Publishers (UK) Ltd for 'Smells' from *Chimney Smoke* by Christopher Morley, Methuen & Co;
A. & C. Black for 'The Spectre on the Moor' by Jack Prelutsky from *The Headless Horseman Rides Tonight*;
Valerie Bloom for 'Don' Go Ova Dere';
Adrienne Brady for 'The Wind is Angry' from *Footnotes* 31, 1984, Schools' Poetry Association;
Cadbury Ltd for 'An Old Derelict Station' by Patrick Humphris from *Cadbury's Second Book of Children's Poetry*, and 'The Boxer' by Emma Payne and 'Dear Sir' by Stephen Dow from *Cadbury's Third Book of Children's Poetry*;
Laura Cecil on behalf of The James Reeves Estate for 'Slowly' from *James Reeves: the complete poems*;
Collins Publishers for 'Christmas Thank You's' from *Swings and Roundabouts* by Mick Gowar;
Wendy Cope for 'Kenneth';
Stanley Cook for 'The Smell That It Is', 'The Four-Masted Hedge' and 'A simile riddle';
Pie Corbett for 'It was...' and 'For Sale';
Nigel Cox for 'The River Cinquains', 'View from the Window' and 'Snapshots: Devon in April';
Chris Darwin for 'Gran's' from *Voices*, Commonword Ltd;
Andre Deutsch Ltd. for 'Nothing Much' from *Quick Let's Get Out Of Here* by Michael Rosen and 'Late last night' from *Wouldn't You Like To Know* by Michael Rosen;
Berlie Doherty for 'I Hear...' and 'Mushrooms';
Eric Finney for 'Wish You Were Here';
Frank Flynn for 'Have You?';
David Higham Associates Ltd on behalf of Eleanor Farjeon for 'It was Long Ago' from *Silver Sand and Snow*, Michael Joseph;
Philip Gross for 'In the Rush Hour Traffic Jam';
Hamish Hamilton Ltd. for extract from *The Cold Flame* by James Reeves;
David Harmer for 'Happy Birthday';
Geoffrey Holloway for 'Gale', 'Giraffe', 'With the Dog' and two haiku;
John Johnson on behalf of Max Fatchen for 'A postcard poem' and 'Bang On';
James Kirkup for 'Reflection', 'Haiku' and 'Comparisons';
John Kitching for 'Snapshot', 'In Good Taste' and two haiku;
Lorrimer Publishing Ltd. for 'Murder Story' by Andrew Rawlinson from *Mindplay*, ed. John Starkey;
Shelagh McGee for 'Wanted — a Witch's Cat' from *What Witches Do* by Shelagh McGee, Prentice-Hall, Inc.;
Macmillan Publishing Company, NY for 'Swift Things Are Beautiful' from *Away Goes Sally* by Elizabeth Coatsworth. Copyright © 1934 by Macmillan Publishing Company, renewed 1962 by Elizabeth Coatsworth Beston;
Wes Magee for 'Sunday Morning';
Judith Nicholls for 'Nice Work', 'Orders', 'Superstitions' and 'Personal';
Gareth Owen for 'Den to Let';
Penguin Books Ltd for 'The Lane' from *Please, Mrs Butler* by Allen Ahlberg, Kestrel Books. Copyright © 1983 by Allen Ahlberg;
Alastair Reid for 'Sounds';
Ian Serraillier for 'How Happily She Laughs';
Derek Stuart for 'December Day', 'It's Raining Cats and Dogs' and 'I Remember';
A.P. Watt Ltd on behalf of Lady Herbert for 'At the Theatre' from *Open That Door* by A.P. Herbert.

Every effort has been made to trace all the copyright holders but if any have been inadvertently overlooked the publishers will be pleased to make the necessary arrangement at the first opportunity.

1: I Remember...

The poems in this section each describe memories of some kind. In the first three poems Eleanor Farjeon, David Harmer and Derek Stuart write about memories of particular incidents. In the poem *Gran's*, Chris Darwin writes about a person of whom he was very fond and in *The Four-masted Hedge* Stanley Cook remembers a place where he used to play.

It was Long Ago

I'll tell you, shall I, something I remember?
Something that still means a great deal to me.
It was long ago.

A dusty road in summer I remember,
A mountain, and an old house, and a tree
That stood, you know,

Behind the house. An old woman I remember
In a red shawl with a grey cat on her knee
Humming under a tree.

She seemed the oldest thing I can remember,
But then perhaps I was not more than three.
It was long ago.

I dragged on the dusty road, and I remember
How the old woman looked over the fence at me
And seemed to know

How it felt to be three, and called out, I remember
'Do you like bilberries and cream for tea?'
I went under the tree

And while she hummed, and the cat purred, I remember
How she filled a saucer with berries and cream for me
So long ago,

Such berries and such cream as I remember
I never had seen before, and never see
Today, you know.

And that is almost all I can remember,
The house, the mountain, the grey cat on her knee,
Her red shawl, and the tree.

And the taste of the berries, the feel of the sun I remember,
And the smell of everything that used to be
So long ago,

Till the heat on the road outside again I remember,
And how the long dusty road seemed to have for me
No end, you know.

That is the farthest thing I can remember.
It won't mean much to you. It does to me.
Then I grew up, you see.

ELEANOR FARJEON

Talking and writing

1 What is the incident the poet describes in this poem? Why does that particular incident mean so much to the poet?

2 a) What pictures did you form in your mind as you read the poem? Think about the mountain, the house, the tree, the woman and the cat. Tell each other about what you 'saw' as you read the poem.

    b) Talk about the feeling you got as you read this poem. Pick out the words and phrases Eleanor Farjeon uses which tell you that the incident was a very pleasant experience for her.

3 Think about some of your earliest memories. Choose an incident that you remember because it was particularly pleasant. Make some notes about it, then try to write a poem about it. Do not necessarily include in your poem all the details you jot down about the incident; select the ones that enable you to convey to the reader what made that incident such a pleasant and memorable one for you.

4 Look at the pattern of the poem. Notice how the first line of each verse ends with the phrase 'I remember' and how the second line of each verse ends with the same rhyme. What do you notice about the third line of each verse?

    Think about a time when you achieved something and felt very pleased with yourself, perhaps because you won something, made something you were proud of or learned to do something, such as to ride a bicycle, to swim or to fly a kite.

(cont'd)

Draft a poem about your memories of your achievement, using a similar pattern to the one Eleanor Farjeon uses. Here is the first verse of such a poem:

> I'll tell you, shall I, something I remember?
> Something I did that meant a great deal to me
> The day I learned to skate...

Note: Do not worry if you find you cannot make the second line of each verse rhyme, as Eleanor Farjeon does. Remember, it is far more important for the poem to say what you want it to say and for it to make sense than it is for it to rhyme.

Happy Birthday

My father's smile
streamed through the window,
a bright red football
as glossy as sunlight
burning his hands.

I was eight for the first time
that day, for a year
I could be older
run faster, jump higher
talk louder and sing

brave pirate shanties
out of the tree-tops
as I swarmed down
the rigging of branches
gritting my teeth.

Later that day
I won the Cup Final,
two minutes to go
and I scored the goal,
brought back the Cup

brought back the football
deflated and lifeless,
the sun punctured
on the rosebush goalpost,
burning my hands.

DAVID HARMER

Talking and writing

1 Think about the poem and its title. Is the memory described in the poem a pleasant or an unpleasant one? Is this a happy poem or a sad poem? Give reasons for your answer.

2 Talk about the words and phrases David Harmer uses to describe
   a) how the father felt as he gave the son his birthday gift;
   b) the new football;
   c) the boy's excitement at being eight years old;
   d) the game the boy played with the new ball;
   e) what happened to the ball.
In groups, discuss which words and phrases in the poem each of you finds the most effective. Which verse do you think is best? Say why.

3 Think about birthdays, Christmases and other festivals when you are given presents. Choose one particular one that stands out in your memory for some reason, perhaps because you were given something you had really longed to have or because something unexpected happened or because, like the boy's in the poem, the gift you were given was soon broken. Use the memory as the starting point for a poem. Work at drafting the poem, experimenting with words and phrases until you find the ones that are most effective for your purpose.

I Remember

I remember
the day my father
went up in the attic
and put his foot
through the ceiling
of my brother's bedroom.
There was plaster everywhere.
Mum collapsed on the bed
and howled with laughter,
pointing at Dad's leg
dangling through the hole,
while Dad struggled and swore
and thrashed about
until finally
the other foot
came crashing through
and Mum laughed so much
she rolled off the bed
and fell on the floor.

JOHN FOSTER

Writing

Try it yourself. Write your own 'I remember' poem about an incident that happened at home, at school, on holiday or while you were out playing with friends. Either base the poem on an incident that actually happened or, if you would prefer to do so, use your imagination and make up an incident — it can be as amusing and far-fetched an incident as you want!

Gran's

I loved me gran,
Me dad's mam.
She was different from me mam's mam,
Me other gran.
She always baked cake with currants in.
Her hands messy with flour
She wiped on her pinny
Before she sipped her Guinness,
And gave me some.
She had a budgie,

Always sitting on the sideboard mirror,
Droppings dropping into a saucer ashtray,
Just missing the only photo of me grandad,
With his cap on the side of his head.
I used confetti once
To try and clean it,

But it bit me finger.
Still I loved me gran's budgie,
And I loved me gran even more,
That's me dad's mam.

But, me mam's mam,
Me other gran,
She chased me with a poker,
And shouted and swore at me,
But that must have been
Because I was cheeky.
She had a dog called
"Where are yer".
It was looked after better than me;
She'd put its dinner out, and shout,
"Where are yer"
And this dog would come from nowhere.
I stood on its paw once;
It bit me,
And left a tooth in me leg.
I cried,
I had to have a needle,
I cried again.
I went back to kick it
But I didn't,
It might have left all its teeth in me,
But I did throw stones at it.
She never had a photo of me other grandad,
I never saw him,

Maybe she chased him with a poker.

CHRIS DARWIN

Talking and writing

1 Chris Darwin's poem is about his memories of two people in his family — his two grans. What impression do you get of a) his dad's mam b) his mam's mam?

2 Notice how Chris Darwin lets you know what his grans were like by describing how they behaved towards him and the pets they kept and how they treated them, rather than by attempting to describe their physical appearances. He picks out two or three significant memories about each of his grans, which enable you to understand what sort of people they were.

Choose any adult who has been close to you and whom you have felt strongly about. Jot down some of your memories about the person. Then, think carefully about what the person is like, what your feelings about the person are and what impression of the person you would want to give when you write about them. Look at the memories you have jotted down, select those which capture most accurately the person's character and your feelings about them and build up a poem about the person using those memories.

3 Write an 'I remember' poem about any person who has made an impression on you because they either dressed, behaved or spoke in a particular way. Think, for example, about people you have seen in shops, cafés and restaurants, people you have met in crowds, standing in queues or on journeys, people you have heard talking on the radio or seen on TV. You could, if you wished, create an imaginary person by mixing together some of your memories of real people.

In this poem Stanley Cook writes about a place where he and his friends used to play.

The Four-masted Hedge

I remember the four great willow trees
In line in the hedge, four tall masts
Of a sailing ship, their branches spread
Out over a sea of grass like yards,
The twisted bark at their base rubbed smooth
By our climbing so often aloft.
In their highest branches on windy days
You felt it needed only a stronger gust
To break the soil above a buried hull
And a resurrected ship to set sail.
The day before they were felled, abandoning ship,
We dropped a last time from the lowest branches
Into the flowing tide of summer grass.
Today a fifteen-storey block of flats
Stands where the deck was and fills the air
Where in the Spring the sails of leaves unfurled.

STANLEY COOK

Talking and writing

1 Stanley Cook thinks of the four great willow trees, where he played as a boy, as the masts of a ship, and throughout the poem he develops this idea. Pick out all the words and phrases he uses to convey the idea that the trees were a ship.

2 When a writer compares one thing with another and

writes as though one object actually *is* the object to which it is being compared, we say that he is using a 'metaphor'. If the writer uses a metaphor at the start of a poem and then develops the idea through the whole poem, as Stanley Cook does, we say that he is using an 'extended metaphor'.

Think of a place where you used to play. What sort of games did you play there? What did you imagine the place was? Tell a partner as much about the place as you can remember. Is it still the same now as it was when you used to play there, or has it changed in any way, just as the place Stanley Cook describes in his poem has changed?

Write a poem about your memories of a place where you used to play. Think about what impression of the place you want to give and choose those details to include in your description which will most help you to give that impression. If you want, try to develop an extended metaphor. Here is an attempt to do so:

> The shed was our Aladdin's cave.
> In it we kept our priceless treasures —
> A coin we found in Johnson's field,
> The whitened jawbone of a sheep,
> Our penknives and our bows and arrows,
> Stored in a cardboard chest,
> Camouflaged by a coat
> We borrowed from a scarecrow.

3 Write a poem about a place — perhaps a house, perhaps a room — which you remember very clearly because you were very happy there. Develop the poem in such a way that the reader can understand why you have such happy memories of that particular place.

4 Write a poem describing your memories of a place which frightened you.

2: Comparison Poems

In our everyday life, we frequently use language to make comparisons. For example, we sometimes say that an object is as white as snow or as light as a feather; or we may say that something was done as quick as a flash.

Work in groups and make a collection of common comparisons that we use in our everyday speech and writing.

Then, as a class, discuss your lists. Do you agree that most of the expressions on your lists have lost some of their effectiveness, because they have been used so often? Did you include any comparisons on your lists that are more unusual and less commonly used and, therefore, more effective than the others?

When an expression has been used so often that it has lost some of its effectiveness, we say that it has become a cliché. As you work through this unit, try to avoid using comparisons that are clichés and to produce comparisons that are effective because they are unusual and original. An original comparison can bring language alive in a way that a cliché cannot.

Simile poems

A simile is an expression in which one thing is compared to another; usually the comparison is introduced by the words 'as' or 'like'. For example:

as bold as brass
the thorn was like a dagger's point.

THE SIMILES GAME

Work with a partner. The object of the game is to give you a chance to produce some imaginative similes. The basic aim is to match the two different halves of the similes given in columns A and B. The idea is for you to make your own new similes. There are no right or wrong answers. There are simply a number of interesting possibilities from which you can choose the combinations that strike you as being the most effective. Do not be afraid to suggest some unusual combinations.

Note: If you want, you can use the same expression more than once.

When you have finished, join up with two other pairs and show each other your similes. Each choose one simile that someone else has thought of, which you think is effective, and explain why you chose that particular one.

A
As sharp as
The gymnast moves like
As cold as
The mist is like
As slippery as
The rhino's hide is like
As dangerous as
An angry teacher is like
As frightening as
The smoke from a volcano is like
As hard as
A dinosaur's tooth is like
As loud as
The dungeon wall feels like
As quick as
A clap of thunder is like
As bright as
A graceful skater is like
As cunning as
A young dancer is like

B
a slab of steel
a lion's roar
a drifting cloud
a prowling leopard
a swooping swallow
an eagle's eye
a silver snowflake
a witch's handshake
a wasp's sting
a giant's laughter
the howl of a hungry wolf
a leaping salmon
a butcher's knife
a dragon's breath
a block of ice
the skin of a statue
a snorting buffalo
a grey curtain
a shivering shadow
an iron spike

Now that you have got the idea of what a simile is, try to write a poem in which you include at least one simile. Either choose a subject of your own or write on one of the subjects from this list:

*Kangaroo   Forest   Dusk   Laughter   Fireworks   Lake
Bulldozer   Boat   Panther   Snowstorm   Volcano   Footsteps*

Begin by jotting down some ideas. Then, think carefully about what you want your poem to say about your subject. Which details and characteristics of the subject are you going to focus on? Build up your poem around those particular features.

A SIMILE RIDDLE

In the next poem, Stanley Cook uses a series of similes to present a riddle:

Like the white curls from a gigantic beard
Drifting across the barber's shop floor
In the breeze from the open door;
Like the broken parts of the ice floe
Afloat on the blue of the ocean,
Drifting southward from the Pole;
Like a heavily laden treasure fleet
In a light wind on a calm sea,
Hardly moving with all sails set;
Like suds of foam from a waterfall
That lathers the rocks at its foot,
Gliding over a tranquil pool;
Like wool from a fleece,
Like smoke from a fire,
Like islands in the sky.

STANLEY COOK

Talking and writing

1 Can you work out what is the subject of the poem? If you had to give the poem a title, what would it be?

2 Which of the similes that Stanley Cook uses do you think is the most effective? Say why.

3 Write a simile riddle poem of your own. Bear in mind that when you are writing such a poem, the comparisons you make must be accurate and appropriate, as Stanley Cook's are. If the comparisons you make are too unusual, you may mislead people and suggest wrong solutions to your riddle.

Note: A simile riddle poem does not have to consist of a particular number of similes. It can consist of whatever number of similes you choose.

THE CONNECTIONS GAME

Here is another word game. The aim of the connections game is to get you to think up unusual comparisons.

Begin by dividing a piece of paper into two columns and in each column write down a list of common nouns. The nouns can be in any particular order, but they should be as varied as possible, rather than just two lists of words that are connected with the same subjects. For example, don't just write down a list of animals' names and a list of words to do with, say, football or computers. Instead, make lists of words that are totally unconnected in any way. Put down about ten words in each list.

Here is the start of two such lists:

trumpet	lamppost
butterfly	postcard
basket	car
kettle	hammer

When you have drawn up your lists, look at the words you have put side by side in the two columns. Ask yourself the question: What is the connection between these two objects? For example:

Why is a trumpet like a lamppost?
Why is a butterfly like a postcard?
Why is a basket like a car?

Now, think of some answers to each of the questions. Do not worry about how absurd or ridiculous the answer is. The important thing is to make a connection between the two objects.

For example, here is an answer to one of the questions: a basket sits on a shelf like a car sits in a garage, they both carry things, people use them for a while then leave them lying idle, they are both solid and tough and can take knocks.

Then, see if you can use the connections you have made between the two objects to produce a comparisons poem. Here is an example:

> The battered basket sits on the kitchen shelf
> like a car in a garage,
> idly wondering, as it waits
> for busy hands to snatch it up,
> when its next journey will be
> and who it will have to carry.

Note: Sometimes it can be hard to see comparisons between objects which appear to be very different. But don't just give up, get your friends to help you. Be prepared to suggest ideas to other people and to borrow ideas from them.

Comparisons

I was thinking it was a dead leaf
blowing slowly along the path—
then I saw it was a fieldmouse.

I was thinking the village pond
had red flowers growing out of it—
then I saw they were Coca Cola cans.

POETRY 2

I was thinking it was a green frog
panting by the side of the slimy pool—
then I saw it was a wind-stirred bubble gum wrapper.

I was thinking it was a seagull
flying and hanging on the autumn wind—
then I saw it was only a bit of greasy chip paper.

I was thinking it was a melting snowflake
on the dark windowpane last night—
then I saw it was the waning moon.

I was thinking it was a girl waving to me
from an upper room, with a yellow handkerchief—
then I saw she was just washing the window.

—I was thinking reality was better
than illusion, than what I'd thought I'd seen.
But then I saw they were equal, and part of each other.

JAMES KIRKUP

Talking and writing

1 In pairs, talk about the first six verses of the poem. Which of the comparisons James Kirkup makes do each of you think is the most effective? Say why.

2 Discuss the meaning of the final verse.

3 Try it yourself. Write a comparisons poem using the same verse pattern as James Kirkup has used in his poem. Here is a verse from such a poem:

> I was thinking it was a hedgehog
> snuffling and rooting for grubs beside the pail—
> then I saw it was only an old scrubbing brush.

Metaphor poems

A metaphor is another type of expression in which a comparison is made. In this case the comparison is made by saying that one object actually *is* another object, or that it possesses the features of another object, rather than by saying it is like another object. Here are some examples of metaphors:
   a ship's anchor is an iron claw
   a mirror is a deep pool
   a telephone is an unscheduled alarm clock
Metaphors, like the ones above, can be expanded into short poems. Here are two examples:

The Sausage

The sausage is a cunning bird
With feathers long and wavy;
It swims about the frying pan
And makes its nest in gravy.

ANON

POETRY 2

The Garden Hose

In the grey evening
I see a long green serpent
With its tail in the dahlias.

It lies in loops across the grass
And drinks softly at the
faucet.

I can hear it swallow.

BEATRICE JANOSCO

Writing

Try it for yourself. Write a short metaphor poem. Either choose your own subject or write on one of the following subjects:

train   bonfire   fingerprints   headache   hoover   saw
bubblegum   ice-lolly   a slab of toffee   pigeons.

COMPARISON POEMS 21

In the next poem, two metaphors are used, the ideas being more fully developed than in a short metaphor poem. We say that the poet is using an 'extended metaphor'.

The Wind is Angry

The wind is angry —
he's been in a rage all night,
stamping his feet, bellowing
and finally breaking out.
In morning light he gallops,
at full tilt, round the house
charging at the walls,
pulling at the thatch
and beating with clenched fists
against the windows.
Even now, he's thrusting
icy fingers through crevices
and under doors.

The house is tired
and slightly bored;
she watches with listless eyes,
sighs — settles on her haunches
and entrenches herself still more.

ADRIENNE BRADY

Finally, here is a poem in which a number of metaphors and similes are used:

Gale

Raspberry canes are pooled flamingos.
A silver birch squirms like a limbo dancer.
Somebody's nicked the sky's spigot.
Somebody's mugging the last roses.

Rain's a crossfire, swirled battalions.
Wind bustles the cypress, water's up
from a punctured main, undercuts the teazle
whose busbys stagger, grenadiers in a trap.

Leaves pitch out of trees like snipers.
Brown as a ratpack, a runaway nag,
the foam-slavered beck belts on.
The moon's mothballs, they've water-cannoned the sun.

Useless to batter the slumped barometer.
All one can do is watch, wonder.
This mad dog with its aniseed rag
will quit when it likes, no sooner.

GEOFFREY HOLLOWAY

COMPARISON POEMS 23

Talking and writing

1 Talk about Adrienne Brady's poem. a) Pick out all the words and phrases she uses to develop the idea that the wind is angry; b) pick out all the words and phrases she uses to suggest the fatigue and boredom of the house.

2 Pick out a) the metaphors b) the similes Geoffrey Holloway uses in his poem. Which do you think are the most effective ones? Say why.

3 Which poem do you prefer — *The wind is angry* or *Gale*? Say why.

4 Try it yourself.

a) Write a poem based on a single extended metaphor. Either use one of the first lines suggested below or an idea of your own:

    Winter is an icy cage
    Schools in the holidays are deserted museums
    Sleep is a heavy curtain
    Toothache is a torturer
    Autumn leaves are dancers

b) Write a poem in which you use a number of similes and metaphors. Either choose a subject of your own or write on one of these subjects:

Sea   Desert   Market   Zoo   Fairground   Hallowe'en.

3: Advice and Warning Poems

Beware...

'Beware the Jabberwock, my son!
The jaws that bite, the claws that snatch!'

LEWIS CARROLL

The Spectre on the Moor

In the ghostly, ghastly silence
of the misty misty moor
a phosphorescent spectre
sets upon its twilight tour,
searching for some hapless victim —
it will find one, oh be sure.

It swirls about the vapours
of the luminescent mist
with its tendrils slowly writhing,
deadly purpose in each twist,
and its grasp is cold and final,
not a creature can resist.

Do not go there in the twilight,
do not heed its dread allure.

It will hold you and enfold you
in such ways you can't endure,
till you never leave the spectre
on the misty misty moor.

JACK PRELUTSKY

Talking and writing

1 Work with a partner. Invent an imaginary creature that lives in one of the following places:
   in a slimy, stinking sea-cave
   in a cold and icy cavern
   on a dark and desolate hillside
   deep in the forest's shadows
   in a foul and filthy hovel.
Imagine that one of you has seen the creature and its lair. Role-play a scene in which a TV reporter interviews her/him and asks for a description of the creature and its lair. Before you begin, make a list of questions that the reporter is going to ask.

2 Write a poem in which you describe the creature and its lair and warn people how dangerous the creature is.

Poem

In the stump of the old tree, where the heart
has rotted out,/there is a hole the length of a
man's arm, and a dank pool at the/bottom of it
where the rain gathers, and the old leaves turn
into/lacy skeletons. But do not put your hand
down to see, because

in the stumps of old trees, where the hearts
have rotted out,/there are holes the length of a
man's arm, and dank pools at the/bottom where
the rain gathers and old leaves turn to lace, and
the/beak of a dead bird gapes like a trap. But do
not put your/hand down to see, because

in the stumps of old trees with rotten hearts
where the rain/gathers and the laced leaves and
the dead bird like a trap, there/are holes the
length of a man's arm, and in every crevice of
the/rotten wood grow weasels' eyes like
molluscs, their lids open/and shut with the tide.
But do not put your hand down to see, because

in the stumps of old trees where the rain
gathers and the/trapped leaves and the beak,
and the laced weasels' eyes, there are/holes the
length of a man's arm, and at the bottom a
sodden bible/written in the language of rooks.
But do not put your hand down/to see, because

in the stumps of old trees where the hearts
have rotted out there are holes the length of a

man's arm where the weasels are/trapped and
the letters of the rook language are laced on
the/sodden leaves, and at the bottom there is a
man's arm. But do/not put your hand down to
see, because

   in the stumps of old trees where the hearts
have rotted out/there are deep holes and dank
pools where the rain gathers, and/if you ever put
your hand down to see, you can wipe it in
the/sharp grass till it bleeds, but you'll never
want to eat with/it again.

HUGH SYKES DAVIES

Talking and writing

1 What strange, unpleasant, mysterious things might you touch if you plunged your hand deep into the hollow stump of the tree? Tell each other about the things that you imagined you might feel there as you listened to the poem being read.

2 This is a poem to be chanted. Work in groups of three and prepare either a tape-recording or a presentation of the poem. Use sound effects and music to help to create an atmosphere of mystery and danger. After all the groups have put on their presentations, hold a de-briefing session. Discuss whose presentation worked best and why.

3 Write a similar poem. Either develop an idea of your own or use one of these suggestions:
   Do not follow the track that leads...
   Never go down those steps because...

Do not ask what lies hidden there because...
Do not prise open the lid because...
Do not draw aside the dark curtain because...
Do not unfasten the heavy oak door because...

Superstitions

Wash your hands in the moonlight,
don't step on any crack;
cross your fingers,
cross your toes,
touch wood to keep your luck.

Always watch for black cats,
wear odd socks unawares;
choose sevens or threes,
'Bless you!' when you sneeze,
and never cross on stairs.

Remember these with all you've got;

                    if not........

JUDITH NICHOLLS

Talking and writing

1 Talk about the superstitions Judith Nicholls mentions in her poem. What other superstitions do you know? What things are considered good luck? What things are considered bad luck? Make lists of a) good omens, b) bad omens.

2 Each culture has its own superstitions. For example, did you know that in Italy it is considered unlucky to sleep under a walnut tree? Or that the Chinese believe that a sneeze on New Year's Eve means bad luck throughout the coming year? Use the library to find out more about superstitions in other times and other countries and add them to your list.

3 Write one or two verses of your own, giving advice about superstitions.

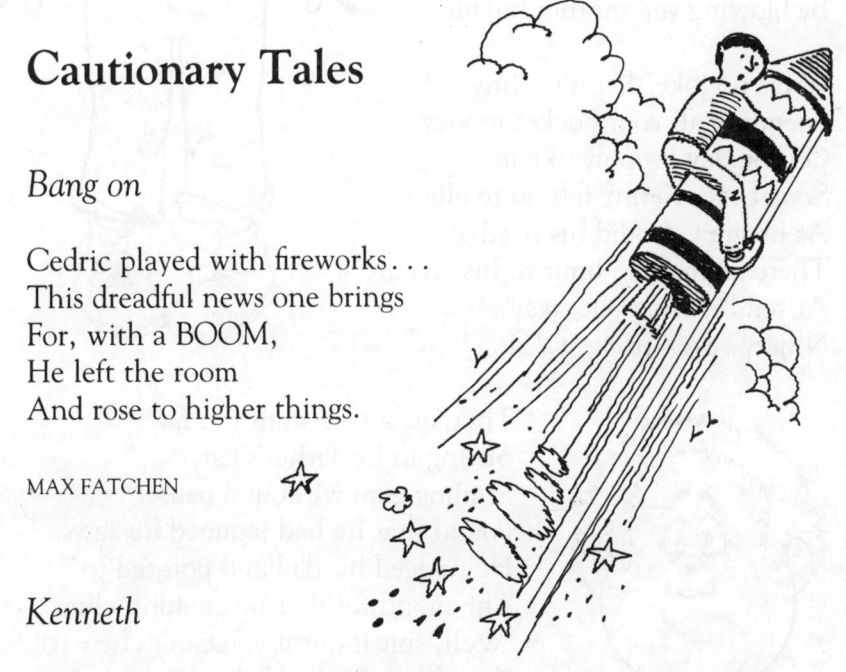

Cautionary Tales

Bang on

Cedric played with fireworks...
This dreadful news one brings
For, with a BOOM,
He left the room
And rose to higher things.

MAX FATCHEN

Kenneth

who was too fond of bubble-gum and met an untimely end.

The chief defect of Kenneth Plumb
Was chewing too much bubble-gum.
He chewed away with all his might,

Morning, evening, noon and night,
Even (oh, it makes you weep)
Blowing bubbles in his sleep.
He simply couldn't get enough!
His face was covered with the stuff
As for his teeth — oh, what a sight!
It was a wonder he could bite.
His loving mother and his dad
Both remonstrated with the lad.
Ken repaid them for their trouble
By blowing yet another bubble.

'Twas no joke. It isn't funny
Spending all your pocket money
On the day's supply of gum —
Sometimes Kenny felt quite glum.
As he grew, so did his need —
There seemed no limit to his greed:
At ten he often put away
Ninety-seven packs a day.

Then at last he went too far —
Sitting in his father's car,
Stuffing gum without a pause,
Found that he had jammed his jaws.
He nudged his dad and pointed to
The mouthful that he couldn't chew.
'Well, spit it out if you can't chew it!'
Ken shook his head. He couldn't do it.
Before long he began to groan —
The gum was solid as a stone.
Dad took him to a builder's yard;
They couldn't help. It was too hard.

ADVICE AND WARNING POEMS

They called a doctor and he said,
'This silly boy will soon be dead.
His mouth's so full of bubble-gum
No nourishment can reach his tum.'

Remember Ken and please do not
Go buying too much you-know-what.

WENDY COPE

Writing

Try it yourself. Write your own cautionary tale. Either develop an idea of your own or use one of the following suggestions and write about:
- a girl who never put her hand over her mouth when she yawned.
- a boy who was so lazy that in the end he could not be bothered to get out of bed or to feed himself.
- Celia Proud, who played her pop-songs much too loud.
- Raymond Gee, who was addicted to TV.
- Sarah Gold, who'd never do as she was told.
- Percy Groom, who never tidied up his room.
- Jenny Bream, who was addicted to ice-crea

4: Senses Poems

Sounds poems

It was...

It was so silent that I heard
my thoughts rustle
like leaves in a paperbag...

It was so peaceful that I heard
the trees ease off their coats of bark...

It was so still that I sensed
a raindrop's shiver
at the groan of the paving stones
as they muscled each other for space...

It was so silent that I heard
the page of a book
whispering to its neighbour,
'Look, he's peering at us again...'

PIE CORBETT

Talking and writing

1 List some of the sounds you might be able to hear if your sense of hearing was much more acute. Here's the start of such a list:

the whisper of a butterfly's wings
the rustle of an eyelash
a blade of grass sighing in the wind.

2 Think about everyday objects and everyday actions and the sounds you might hear if it was extremely quiet. For example:
   the purr of a shirt as an iron smoothes its back
   the groan of a coathanger as it takes the weight of a jacket
   the sigh of an envelope as it is sealed.
What else can you suggest?

3 Try it for yourself. Write your own poem beginning: It was so silent that I could hear...

Many words actually sound like or imitate the noise or action which they describe: words like hiss and purr, shuffle and squirm. Such words are examples of what is called onomatopoeia — their sounds remind us of what they describe.

Writing

1 Work in pairs. Make lists of words that remind you of a) the noises they describe, b) the actions they describe.

2 Choose one of the words from your lists and build up a poem about it. Here is one attempt at such a poem:
   Hissing is...
      a cornered snake
      a burst of steam from a boiling kettle
      air draining from a punctured tyre.

Hissing is...
>   a spiteful cat
>   the glow of a gas-fire on a cold winter's night
>   an angry crowd at a wrestling bout.

Sometimes, when you want to describe a particular sound, it can be hard to find a word that exactly matches the sound. One way of solving the problem is to make up or coin a word. For example, if you wanted to describe the sound a mouse makes as it scratches and scuttles along beneath the floorboards, you could coin the word 'scrutter'. You could write:

>   Beneath the floorboards the scruttering mouse
>   Disturbs the silence of the house.

Sounds

PLOO
is breaking your shoelace.

MRRAAOWL
is what cats really say.

TRIS-TRAS
is scissors cutting paper.

KINCLUNK
is a car going over a manhole cover.

PHLOOPH
is sitting suddenly on a cushion.

CROOMB
is what pigeons murmur to themselves.

NYO-NYO
is speaking with your mouth full.

HARROWOLLOWORRAH
is yawning.

PALOOP
is the tap dripping in the bath.

RAM TAM GEE PICKAGE
is feeling good.

ALASTAIR REID

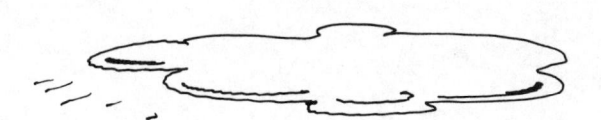

Talking and writing

1 Talk about the sound words that Alastair Reid has invented. Which of the words do you think is the most suitable for the sound it describes?

2 When two objects come into contact it can be difficult to find a word that exactly describes the sound that is made. For example, how would you describe the noise made by a) a knife scraping on a plate, b) a brush sweeping a rug, c) a wet sponge being used to wipe a window pane? Work with a partner and coin some words to describe these sounds.

3 Work on your own, inventing some sound words. Then, as a class, produce a glossary of new sound words, duplicate it and distribute it to other classes. You could invite them to submit new words to consider for a second edition of your glossary and offer a prize for the best suggestion.

SCHOOL SOUNDS

What sounds do you associate with school? Make a list of school sounds. Think of the sounds you hear in the following places: the playground, the corridor, the dining-hall, the classroom, the gym, the craft rooms, the science labs and the music room.

Here is a poem about school sounds:

I Hear......

When I think of school
I hear
High shouts tossed
Like juggled balls in windy yards, and lost
In gutters, treetops, all.
And always, somewhere.
Piano-notes water-fall
And small sharp voices wail.
A monster-roar surges — 'Goal!'.
The bell.
Then doors slam. There's the kick, scuff, stamp of shoes
Down corridors that trap and trail echoes.
Desk-tops thud with books, kit-bags,
A child's ghost screams as her chair's pushed back.

Laughter bubbles up and bursts.
Screech-owl whistles. Quick-fox quarrel-flares.
The voice barks 'QUIET!'
All sit. All wait.
Till scraped chalk shrieks
And whispers creep.
Cough. Ruler crack. Desk creak.
And furtive into the silence comes
A tiny mouse-scrabbling of pens.
Scamper. Stop. Scamper. Stop. Tiptoe
And there, just outside the top window
As if it had never ceased to be
But only needed listening to
A scatter of birdsong, floating free.

BERLIE DOHERTY

Talking and writing

1 This poem is more than just a list of school sounds. Talk about how Berlie Doherty uses a sequence of sounds to describe a sequence of events.

a) Draw a flow-chart of the sequence of events in the poem and by means of arrows indicate the sounds which are mentioned. Here is the start of such a flow-chart:

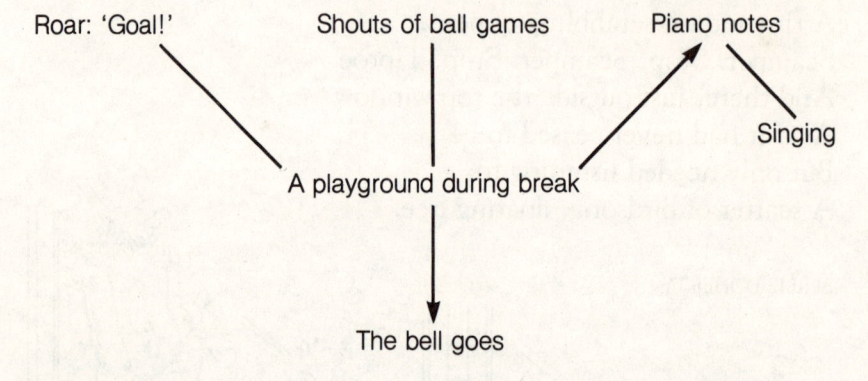

```
Roar: 'Goal!'        Shouts of ball games        Piano notes
        \                    |                      ↗
         \                   |                     /
          \                  |                    Singing
           \                 |
            A playground during break
                             |
                             ↓
                        The bell goes
```

b) When you have completed the flow-chart, talk about the words Berlie Doherty uses in the poem to describe each of the sounds. Pick out the three lines which you think are the most effective and say why.

c) Talk about the last four lines of the poem. How do they fit in with the rest of the poem? Do you think they sum up the 'message' of the poem? If so, what is the message of the poem?

2 Write a poem about the sounds you hear at school at the end of the day. Plan it by drawing a flow-chart of the sequence of events and use arrows to indicate the sounds you would hear. Then, think of words and phrases that effectively describe the sounds you want to include in the poem and start to draft your poem. Don't necessarily include all the ideas from your plan in the poem. Only include the ones that fit in with the way the poem develops as you write it. Try to think of a suitable way to end your poem. Here is the start of such a poem:

> When I think of school at the end of the day
> I hear
> The smack of books closing
> The rattle of pencils in pencil cases
> The slap of satchels being lifted on to desks...

3 Write an *I Hear...* poem about the sounds you hear:
— at a football match, moto-cross meeting, gymnastics competition or any other sporting event;
— at home at a particular time of the day;
— on a visit to a place such as a swimming pool, ice-rink, circus or amusement arcade;
— at a place such as a railway station, an airport, a building site, a supermarket or a factory.

Either use one of these ideas or an idea of your own. Plan your poem by jotting down some notes or by drawing a flow-chart. Try to include at least one simile or metaphor (see pages 12 and 19).

SOUNDS OF A SOLDIER'S LIFE

In this extract from a novel called *The Cold Flame* the poet James Reeves uses a list of sounds to suggest the type of life a soldier has led:

> Five and twenty summers, unmarched, unrolled like an old trooper's windy tale in a hedge-inn's corner — what sounds would they bring? Trumpets in the drenched mornings; kettle-drums; laughter and swearing of raw-voiced youngsters; rumbling and growling of veterans; the neigh of horses; bells in pious hill villages; bells from town steeples and huzzas for relieving soldiers; carters' oaths; singing of milkmaids; commands of stable-lads to whinnying horses; barking of dogs, cackle of hens, squealing of pigs, screaming of cocks in endless line like beacons of sound over counties, countries, nations. Rolling of thunder, rolling of cannon, hooves of cavalry on wooden bridges; jaunty sharp tunes of fifes; familiar bawdy songs, and the groans of wounded men, groans of the dying; whining of children and sobs of the inconsolable. Under it all, unrolled from the five-and-twenty years, was the beat of boots. Left, left, left right left. Soldiers must curse and sing; women must rail and weep; animals scream and brawl. The march must go on, endlessly nearing an end.

Talking and writing

1 What impression of a soldier's life does this passage give you? Say why.

2 a) Pick out the words and phrases which you think are the most effective in giving you an impression of the soldier's life.

b) The description is about 175 words long. If you had to shorten it, which phrases would you include? which phrases would you leave out? Rework it to try to give an impression of the soldier's life using no more than 50 words. When you have finished, compare your versions and decide whose is best and why.

3 Write a poem in which you use the sounds of a person's life to suggest the type of life they lead. Either develop an idea of your own or write about one of the following: a fire officer, a long-distance lorry driver, a police officer, a cowboy, a cook, a shop assistant, a sailor, a caretaker, a schoolteacher.

Smells and tastes

TYPES OF SMELL

Work with a partner. The aim is to match the words you can use to describe particular smells given in column A with the smells listed in column B. There are twelve words in column A, but there are eighteen in column B, because there are lots of possibilities and no right or wrong answers. Since you are trying to find the most appropriate word to describe each smell, you can use a word from column A more than once.

When you have finished, join up with another pair. Show

them your list, explain your choices and discuss any differences
between your list and theirs.

A	B
fragrance	damp seaweed
stench	a jar of pickles
whiff	fish on a fishmonger's slab
aroma	the slices of a lemon
stink	a lawn that has just been mown
perfume	a pair of trainers
odour	furniture polish
pungency	a pile of wood shavings
scent	a bottle of disinfectant
bouquet	wood smoke from a bonfire
tang	exhaust fumes from a motor-bike
reek	a bunch of daffodils
	a freshly-baked loaf of bread
	hamburgers being grilled
	garden compost
	a powder compact
	a pan of milk that has boiled over
	burning rubber

Smells

Why is it that the poets tell
So little of the sense of smell?
These are the odours I love well:

The smell of coffee freshly ground;
Or rich plum pudding, holly crowned;
Or onions fried and deeply browned.

The fragrance of a fumy pipe;
The smell of apples, newly ripe;
And printers' ink on leaden type.

Woods by moonlight in September
Breathe most sweet; and I remember
Many a smoky camp-fire ember.

Camphor, turpentine, and tea,
The balsam of a Christmas tree,
These are whiffs of gramarye...
A ship smells best of all to me!

CHRISTOPHER MORLEY

The Smell That It Is

Has it the sharp sour smell of cheese
The grocer slices in triangular pieces
Or the smoky smell of tea leaves
Let out by lifting the lid
Of the flowery tin where it hid
Till teatime in the kitchen?

The sweetness of blackberries
Country children gather
Crushed into a jar
Or hawthorn and elderberry flowers
Frothing like freshly poured
Coca-cola round a straw?

The musty smell of hair
Dried beside the fire
Or the tiny smell of scent
Parcelled in a bottle
For a birthday present?

The dark brown smell of rotting leaves
Trodden into puddles beneath the trees?
Or is there some other smell
You remember better
Than any of these?

STANLEY COOK

Talking and writing

1 Go through Christopher Morley's poem. Which of the words from column A would you choose to describe each of the smells he mentions?

2 Do you share Christopher Morley's views? Make lists of a) your favourite smells, b) smells you can't stand. (*Note:* 'Gramarye' means 'magic'.)

SENSES POEMS 45

3 Why do you think Christopher Morley says: 'A ship smells best of all'? What smells do you associate with ships? Work with a partner and make a list of ships' smells.

4 Talk about each of the smells Stanley Cook says he remembers. Discuss the words he uses to describe each particular smell. Which of the smells do you think he describes most accurately and vividly?

5 Stanley Cook uses a variety of adjectives to describe the different smells — sharp, sour, musty, tiny, dark brown. Work in pairs. Go through the lists you made of smells you like and smells you dislike. Can you think of a suitable adjective to describe each one? To help you, here is a list of some of the adjectives you could use: rich, sharp, acrid, sweet, bitter, bright, dark, sour, fragrant, pungent, thin, thick, musty, comforting, exotic, foul. The list could be very long indeed. As well as using some of these suggestions, try to think of other words that more accurately describe the smells on your lists.

6 Write a poem about the smells you like and dislike. You could arrange it so that you write alternately about a smell you like, then a smell you dislike. Here is the start of such a poem:

> I like the warm summery smell
>   of a field of new-mown hay.
> I can't stand the stale odour of tobacco smoke
>   that lingers over a dirty ash-tray...

7 Write a poem like Stanley Cook's about four or more smells that you remember clearly because each of them is so different from the others. As you draft your poem, try to find words that clearly convey to the reader the distinctive nature of each smell.

Tastes

In Good Taste

I sit for twenty minutes
And suck my Cyprus grape.
I gently press its greenness
But keep its green-egg shape.

However deep my hunger,
However dry my thirst,
I've bet myself a fortune
I won't let my grape burst.

Then, when the time is ripest,
The second I most please,
I give my warmly juicy grape
The softest tonguey squeeze.

The sugared juice just syrups out
A trickle on my lips —
This is the taste of heaven:
Don't even mind the pips.

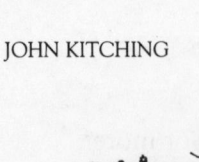

JOHN KITCHING

Talking and writing

1 Are there any foods you try to eat as slowly as you can so that the taste lingers in your mouth? Tell each other about them and how you try to make them last.

2 Make lists of tastes you like and tastes you dislike.
Talk about each one in turn and try to find a way of describing it by discussing these questions:

   a) What sort of taste is it — bitter or sweet? sharp or bland? savoury or sugary? tangy or plain?

   b) Could you use any of the words we use to describe the texture of things to describe that particular taste? For example, is it hard or soft? rough or smooth?

   c) Is the taste thick or thin? warm or cold? light or heavy? pale or dark? weak or strong? sharp or blunt?

   d) If you had to choose a colour to describe the taste, what colour would you choose? Say why.

   e) Do you associate the taste with anything? Does it remind you of anything? Can you compare it to anything?

3 Use the notes you have made in answer to question 2 and write a poem about tastes. Here is the start of such a poem:

> I like the smooth, slithery taste of blancmange,
>   cool and creamy...

In the next poem, Berlie Doherty uses all the five senses, not just the sense of taste, in order to describe what mushrooms are like:

Mushrooms

Bald things,
Thrust heads through soil
And commune
Pale and quiet
In their own damp smell.

Their stems pop when they're plucked
Their skin peels away
Their peat-cool flesh is soft.

Fried in hot butter
They grow plump as the slugs
That slithered round their stems,
They gleam with oozed sweat.

And when they're bitten
They burst
Spilling juices
That taste of grass
And fresh dew trodden in by horses
And foxy woodland
And the deep moist brown dark earth.

BERLIE DOHERTY

SENSES POEMS 49

Talking and writing

1 Pick out the places in the poem where Berlie Doherty uses the senses of a) sight, b) sound, c) touch, d) smell, e) taste.

2 a) Which of the four parts of the poem do you prefer? Say why.
   b) Which phrase in the poem do you think is the most effective?

3 Work in pairs. Each choose a fruit or a vegetable that you particularly like. Talk about all its features and make notes on a) what it looks like, b) what it feels like, c) what it smells like, d) what its taste is like, e) what it reminds you of. Then, write a poem about it. Either develop the poem in your own way or divide it into sections in the way Berlie Doherty has done.

4 Write a poem about a fruit and vegetable stall, using all the five senses to try to describe the various items on display and to capture the atmosphere of the stall.

Frank Flynn's *Have You?* is another kind of senses poem. He presents a series of questions about different sounds, sights and feelings. Each question is followed by an answer in which he compares the sound, sight or feeling to something else.

Have You?

Have you heard the water
As it drips from the tap?
Slow drummer in the sink.

Have you seen the rain
Trickle down your window pane?
Silver snakes in the night.

Have you sheltered from a cloudburst
Beneath a chestnut tree?
Heaven machine-gunning the leaves.

Have you heard the waves crash
On a stormy shore?
A wild music of pebbles.

Have you dived into a pool
On a summer's day?
A blade slicing the silence.

Have you seen a bead of dew
Jewel a daisy's petal?
A diamond in the snow.

Have you touched a spider's web
After a shower of rain?
Splinters of ice in the moonlight.

Have you listened to the rain
Fall gently on a summer's night?
A warm lullaby.

FRANK FLYNN

Talking and writing

1 Work in groups of four. Tell each other which of the comparisons you think is the most effective and say why.

2 Produce a group presentation of the poem. Decide how you can make the presentation as effective as possible. For example, are you each going to read two verses, or are two people going to ask the questions in turn, while two others provide the answers? Can you think of any ways you could present the poem differently in order to make it interesting to listeners?

3 Work on your own and try it yourself. Write your own *Have You?* poem, following the pattern that Frank Flynn uses. Include questions about tastes, smells and touch as well as about sounds and sights.

5: Conversation Poems

Each of the poems in this section consists of part of a conversation. In the first poem a girl is having a conversation with her mother, but the poem presents only what the girl says.

Ta-ra mam

Ta-ra mam
Can you hear me? I'm going out to play.
I've got me playing-out clothes on
and me wellies.
What d'yer say?
Oh! I'm going to the cow-field
I'm going with me mates.
Yes! I know tea's nearly ready.
I promise I won't be late.

Anyway, what we havin'?
Can't I have beans on toast?
What d'yer mean, mam, summat proper?
I ate me dinner (almost).
No, I won't go anywhere lonely,
and I'm going with Chris and Jackie,
so if anyone gets funny
we can all do our karate!

Yer what?
(Oh blimey. Here we go again.)
No, I won't go near the river.
I know we've had too much rain
and I won't go in the newsagent's
trying to nick the sweets.
Yer what, mam? I'm not. Honest.
I'm not trying to give yer cheek.

Wait mam.
Hang on a minute. Chris is here in the hall.
He says summat good's on the telly.
So I think I'll stay in after all!

BRENDA LEATHER

Talking and writing

Work in pairs.
1 Where exactly do you think a) the girl is,
b) the mother is, while the conversation is taking place?

2 Go through the poem and decide at which points the mother speaks. Make a list of the points at which she speaks. Here is the start of such a list:
   i) Between lines 4 and 5.

3 Suggest what the mother says each time she speaks and write down what you think she says.

4 Now, act out the complete conversation with one of you taking the part of the daughter and reading the poem, section by section, and one of you taking the part of the mother and reading out what the mother says.

5 How did it sound? Redraft the mother's part of the conversation in any way you think is necessary, then join up with another pair. Listen to each other's versions of the conversations. Whose sounds better? Why?

Writing

1 Write a similar poem,

a) in which a girl or a boy is upstairs shouting replies to a parent downstairs urging her/him to hurry up. Either make up your own title or call it: *All Right, I'm Coming!*

b) in which a girl or boy, who is looking for something, carries on a conversation with a parent, who refuses to stop what she/he is doing and to join in the search. You could start it:

Hey, mam,
Have you seen my...

2 Work with a partner.

a) Role play a scene in which two young people have a telephone conversation during which one of them tries to persuade the other to do something. In the end, a quarrel develops.

b) Join up with another pair. Show each other your role plays. As you watch, listen carefully to the language used in the conversations and jot down some of the phrases that are used.

c) Draft a telephone conversation poem which presents only one side of the conversation. As you write, think about the words and phrases you used in the role plays and refer to the notes you made.

Here is a poem about a conversation between two children:

Nothing Much

'What did you do on Friday?'
'Nothing much —
I like doing nothing quite often —
like putting on old hats
or drawing forests along the edges
of the newspapers we keep under the sink.
How about you?'

'I showed my mum and dad
what I had made in school that week.
It was a lorry
that works on elastic bands
and my dad said:
"What did you make that thing for?"
I bet he played with it when I went to bed.'

MICHAEL ROSEN

Writing

Try it yourself. Write a poem about a conversation between two children which begins with a question. Either think up your own opening line or use one of these:
    What did you do at the weekend?
    Where are you going for your holidays?
    Did you see that programme last night?
    What are you doing tomorrow afternoon?
    Where did you go last night?

In the next poem, Michael Rosen writes about the sort of misunderstandings that can arise when someone is slightly deaf or doesn't quite hear what you said.

Late Last Night

ME: 'Late last night
        I lay in bed.'
GRAN: 'You lay in lead?'
ME: '"In bed," I said.'
GRAN: 'You led your bed?'
ME: 'I said: "I lay"'
GRAN: 'You lay in bed?
        You should have said.'

MICHAEL ROSEN

Talking and writing

Notice how a conversation poem, such as this, is based on words that rhyme like 'bed', 'lead' and 'said' or that are homonyms, e.g. 'lead' and 'led'. A homonym is a word which has the same sound as another word, but a different meaning. Other examples are: 'sale' and 'sail', 'pair' and 'pear', 'beach' and 'beech'.

Work with a partner and draw up a list of homonyms. Then, try to write a conversation poem in which a misunderstanding develops. Here is another example:

It's Raining Cats and Dogs

MUM: It's raining cats and dogs out there.
GRAN: The dog's out where?
MUM: No, it's raining very hard.
         It's very wet out.
GRAN: The vet's come out.
         Why? Is the dog not well?
MUM: The dog's fine.
GRAN: No, it's not.
         It's raining cats and dogs.

JOHN FOSTER

Finally, here is a poem about a conversation between a boy and his teacher.

Orders

You boy,
GET DOWN from that ceiling at once!
But my chewing gum's stuck, sir...
Why did you bring chewing gum to school?
To fill the hole in my wellies, sir...

Who said you could wear boots in school?
My daps got wet on the field, sir...
Who gave you permission to go on the field?
But nobody had arrived in the classroom, sir...
Why were you in the classroom before I arrived?
Because I wanted to get my chewing gum, sir...
What *is* that mess stuck on the ceiling?
Get it down – AT ONCE!
Teachers!

JUDITH NICHOLLS

Work in pairs

1 Role-play a scene at school in which a teacher catches a girl or a boy doing something wrong. Act out two different scenes, taking it in turns to be the teacher.

2 Think about the different expressions teachers, parents and other adults use to give you orders, instructions and advice. Make lists of a) teachers' sayings, b) parents' sayings. Pick out two sayings from each list which you find very irritating. When you have finished, form groups of four or six and compare your lists.

Writing

1 Write a poem called *Irritating Sayings*. Either think of your own opening or use this one:

   I can't stand the way
   That they always say...

2 Write your own poem called *Orders*. Here are some possible openings:

You, girl!
WHAT do you think you are doing?

ANGELA!
And what, may I ask, is the meaning of this?

Leroy!
COME HERE! Where do you think you are going?

All right,
What have you got there? Bring it up here.

6: Advertisement Poems

Wanted — A Witch's Cat

Wanted — a witch's cat.
Must have vigour and spite,
Be expert at hissing,
And good in a fight,
And have balance and poise
On a broomstick at night.

Wanted — a witch's cat.
Must have hypnotic eyes
To tantalize victims
And mesmerize spies,
And be an adept
At scanning the skies.

Wanted — a witch's cat,
With a sly, cunning smile,
A knowledge of spells
And a good deal of guile,
With a fairly hot temper
And plenty of bile.

Wanted — a witch's cat,
Who's not afraid to fly,
For a cat with strong nerves

ADVERTISEMENT POEMS

The salary's high
Wanted — a witch's cat;
Only the best need apply.

SHELAGH MCGEE

Writing

1 Make a list of the qualities which the advertisement says the witch's cat must have. Then, write a letter from a cat which is answering the advertisement, giving details of its qualities and its previous experience. Make up a name for the cat which is applying and say when it will be available for interview.

2 Write a similar poem advertising for one of the following:
- a sorcerer's serpent
- a conjuror's rabbit
- a pirate's parrot
- a poacher's dog
- a circus flea.

Before you begin to draft your poem, collect some ideas by making a list of the qualities which applicants for the post must have.

3 Write a Wanted poem advertising for one of the following items:
a wizard's wand; a witch's broomstick; a flying carpet; a staff of power; boots of speed; a crystal ball; a sorcerer's spellbook; a cloak of protection.

For Sale

> GENUINE ANTIQUE. One pre-war Grandad. Long mileage but still in good running order. Regularly serviced. Comes complete with NEW TEETH! Fully reconditioned to give good pocket money. Buy now while stock lasts.

PIE CORBETT

Personal

Middle-aged male,
slightly balding,
one eye lost in battle
years ago, but copes.
Friendly nature,
uncomplaining.
Lives simply,
inexpensive tastes,
no ties.
Seeks good home, friendship,
view to permanent relationship.

Contact: Edward Bear, Box 100 (Spare Room)

JUDITH NICHOLLS

Talking and writing

1 Talk about how the advertisements are worded in the 'For Sale' sections in your local newspapers. Then, write an advertisement describing a person who is for sale. Here are some suggestions for the people you could offer for sale: yourself; a brother or a sister; a teacher; a circus clown; a pirate; an alien; a ghost.

2 Write a personal column advertisement poem in which a toy, like Judith Nicholls's bear, describes itself and seeks a new home because it is no longer wanted by its owner. It could be a cuddly toy, a puppet, a toy figure (e.g. a toy soldier, a Smurf, a Dungeons and Dragons figure) or a model of a prehistoric monster or a space creature.

3 Invent an animal cartoon character, e.g. Georgie the Gerbil, Arthur Antelope, Katie the Kangaroo. Imagine that the animal is currently out of work so it is looking for a part in a new TV show or in a new comic. Write a personal column advertisement poem in which it describes its talents and states the type of work it is looking for.

Den to Let

To let
One, self-contained
Detached den.
Accommodation is compact
Measuring one yard square.
Ideal for two eight-year-olds
Plus one small dog,
Or two cats
Or six gerbils.
Accommodation consists of:
One living room
Which doubles as,
Kitchen
Bedroom
Entrance hall
Dining room

Dungeon
Space capsule
Pirate boat
Covered waggon
Racing car
Palace
Aeroplane
Junk room
And look-out post.
Property is southward-facing
And can be found
Within a short walking distance
Of the back door
At bottom of garden.
Easily found in the dark
By following the smell
Of old cabbages and tea bags.
Convenient escape routes
Past rubbish dump
To Seager's Lane
Through hole in hedge
Or into next-door's garden
But beware of next-door's rhinoceros
Who sometimes thinks he's a mongrel.
Construction is of
Sound, corrugated iron
And roof doubles as shower
During rainy weather.
Being partially underground,
Den makes
A particularly effective hiding place
When in a state of war
With older sisters

Brothers
Angry neighbours
Or when you simply want to be alone.
Some repair work needed
To North wall
Where Mr Spence's foot came through
When planting turnips last Thursday.
With den go all contents
Including:
One carpet — very smelly
One tea pot — cracked
One woolly penguin
No beak and only one wing
One, unopened tin
Of sultana pud
One hundred and three Beanos
Dated 1983—1985
And four Rupert annuals.
Rent is free
The only payment being
That the new occupant
Should care for the den
In the manner to which it has been accustomed
And on long Summer evenings
Heroic songs of days gone by
Should be loudly sung
So that old and glorious days
Will never be forgotten.

GARETH OWEN

Writing

Try it yourself. Write a similar type of poem in which you advertise a place. When you have finished, design a poster consisting of your poem and an illustration to go with it.

1 Write a poem called *Secret Hiding-place To Let*. Either write about a secret hiding-place of your own or about a place such as a cellar or an attic, a tree-house or a cave.

2 Write a poem called *Bedroom To Let* in which you advertise your own bedroom. Plan your poem by thinking about all the details of the room you are going to describe, such as its size and shape, how it is decorated, what furniture there is, what the curtains and carpets are like, what pictures there are on the walls. Then, think about your personal possessions — your books, radio and other belongings. Decide what sort of person would like to live in your bedroom, e.g. would it suit someone who is interested in sports or in model-making? Or would it suit someone who is interested in reading or pop music? In your poem, make it clear what sort of person your room would be suitable for.

3 Write an advertisement poem about a school. Call it either *School For Sale*, *Classroom To Let* or *Desk For Hire*.

7: Adjective Poems

The dictionary definition of an adjective is: any word which describes or adds to the meaning of a noun.

A NOUN is the name of anything
As *school* or *garden*, *hoop* or *swing*.
ADJECTIVES tell the kind of noun
As *great*, *small*, *pretty*, *white* or *brown*.

ANON.

THE ADJECTIVE GAME: AUNT AGATHA'S CAT
Aunt Agatha's Cat is a game for the whole class. The aim of the game is to get you to think of as many adjectives as you can, which all start with the same letter of the alphabet.
 The rules are simple. You choose a letter of the alphabet, then you go round the class and each person in turn has to think of an adjective beginning with the letter you have chosen. For example, if you have chosen the letter A, the first person might say: 'Aunt Agatha's cat is an angry cat', then the next person might say 'Aunt Agatha's cat is an active cat' and so on. You keep going until somebody gets stuck or suggests a word which is not an adjective. See how many times you can go round the class for each different letter of the alphabet.
Note: Any adjectives will do, provided they start with the right letter of the alphabet. Don't worry if you think of an adjective that you wouldn't normally use to describe a cat, e.g. you could

say that Aunt Agatha's cat is an 'accurate' cat or an 'alternative' cat.

What are heavy? Sea-sand and sorrow

What are heavy? Sea-sand and sorrow:
What are brief? Today and tomorrow:
What are frail? Spring blossoms and youth:
What are deep? The ocean and truth.

CHRISTINA ROSETTI

Talking and writing

Work in pairs.
1 Choose six adjectives from this list:
   soft   sharp   strong   bright   dull   flat   rough   smooth
   hard   round   long   short   wide   narrow   thin   tall
   large   fat

Draw six columns on a piece of paper. In each column list the names of things that the adjective could be used to describe. Include all kinds of nouns, e.g. abstract nouns such as hope, pain, spite as well as the names of objects. Here is the start of such a list:

Sharp
 thorns
 drawing pins
 spite
 needles

When you have finished, form groups and compare your lists.

2 Try it yourself. Write your own 'What are...' poems. See if you can make your poem rhyme, as Christina Rosetti's does, but don't worry if you can't.

Four Seasons

Spring is showery, flowery, bowery.
Summer: hoppy, choppy, poppy.
Autumn: wheezy, sneezy, freezy.
Winter: slippy, drippy, nippy.

ANON.

Talking and writing

1 *A class calendar poem*
Work together to produce a similar poem about the months of the year. Divide the class into six groups and choose two months for each group to focus on.

In your groups, get each member of the group to draw two columns on a piece of paper and make lists of adjectives you could use to describe each month. Then, compare your lists and make a group choice of four adjectives to describe each month. Write out your suggestions and give them to your teacher.

Ask your teacher to write your suggestions up on the board, then as a class read and discuss the poem you have created. Talk about whether you can improve it in any way, e.g. by cutting out any repetitions, or by altering any words that don't sound quite right or by trying to make it rhyme.

2 Try it yourself. Write a similar poem of your own. Either write a three-line poem: *Times of the Day* (about morning, afternoon and evening) or a seven-line poem about the days of the week. Before you start to draft your poem, collect your ideas together by making lists of adjectives to choose from.

Swift Things are Beautiful

Swift things are beautiful:
Swallows and deer,
And lightning that falls
Bright veined and clear,
Rivers and meteors,
Wind in the wheat,
The strong-withered horse,
The runner's sure feet.

And slow things are beautiful:
The closing of day,
The pause of the wave
That curves downward to spray,
The ember that crumbles,
The opening flower,
And the ox that moves on
In the quiet of power.

ELIZABETH COATSWORTH

Writing

Try it yourself. Write a verse of your own, following the same pattern as Elizabeth Coatsworth's two verses. Either think of a

first line of your own or use one of the following first lines:
Soft things are beautiful...
Frail things are beautiful...
Bright things are beautiful...
Cool things are beautiful...

Descriptive poems are often full of adjectives. Here is an example:

The Whale

Warm and buoyant in his oily mail
Gambols on seas of ice the unwieldy whale,
Wide waving fins round floating islands urge
His bulk gigantic through the troubled surge.

O'er the white wave he lifts his nostril bare,
And spouts transparent columns into the air;
The silvery arches catch the setting beams,
And transient rainbows tremble o'er the streams.

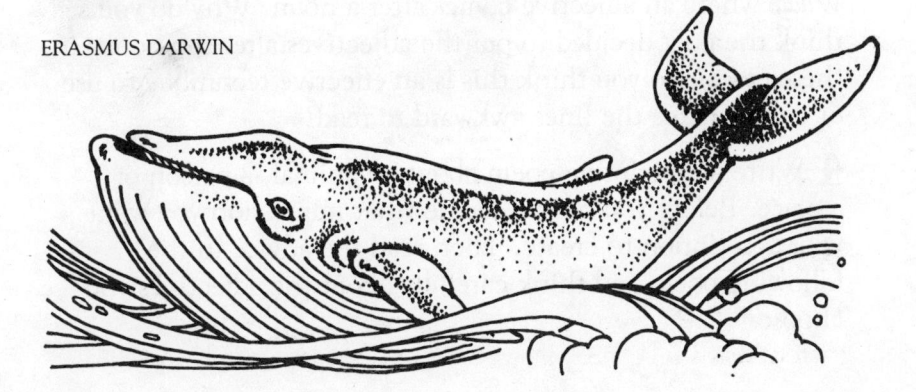

ERASMUS DARWIN

Talking and writing

1 Can you spot the adjectives? There are nine in the first verse and six in the second.
Note: The words formed from verbs known as present participles and past participles can be used as adjectives. The commonest way of forming the present participle is by adding -ing to the stem of the verb e.g. whisper + -ing = whispering. It can be used as an adjective, e.g. the whispering breeze. Similarly, the commonest way of forming the past participle is by adding -ed to the stem of the verb, e.g. frighten + -ed = frightened. It can be used as an adjective, e.g. The frightened mouse cowers in the hedgerow.

What examples of participles used as adjectives are there in the first verse?

2 Which of the adjectives used a) in the first verse, b) in the second verse do you think is the most effective? Say why.

3 The most usual place for an adjective is immediately before the noun it describes, e.g. the unwieldy whale, the white wave. But, sometimes, in order to stress a word, to get the rhythm of a line right or to make a rhyme, a poet may place an adjective after a noun. Find two examples in *The Whale* where an adjective comes after a noun. Why do you think the poet decided to put the adjectives after the nouns in these cases? Do you think this is an effective technique to use or does it make the lines awkward to read?

4 Write a descriptive poem about an animal, a person or a place. Before you begin, decide what impression you want your description to create. Then read the advice in the following poem and think carefully about the adjectives you choose.

Choosing and using adjectives

Nice Work

Never use the word NICE, *our teacher said.*
It doesn't mean a thing!
Try...
beautiful, shining, delicious,
shimmering, hopeful, auspicious,
attractive, unusual, nutritious –
the choice is as long as a string!
But please, *never* use the word NICE,
it just doesn't mean a thing!

[*She's nice, our teacher.*]

JUDITH NICHOLLS

1 Avoid adjectives such as 'nice', 'pretty' and 'sweet'. They have been used so often that they have lost most of their meaning.
2 Don't just choose words from the surface level of your vocabulary, e.g. 'big', 'little'. Instead, experiment with new words. Use a thesaurus to suggest alternatives. But only use a long word if it is appropriate and make sure you understand its exact meaning. If your are unsure, check its meaning in a dictionary.
3 Don't fall into the trap of using too many adjectives, when only one or two would be sufficient. Young writers sometimes make the mistake of overloading their writing with strings of adjectives.

8: Snapshot Poems

A snapshot poem is a poem which, like a photograph, captures a particular scene and describes it at a certain moment in time. A snapshot poem can focus on a place or a person, or on something seen in the poet's imagination. The first poem was written when the writer was aged ten:

An Old Derelict Station

The lonely old station was still,
There was a slight chill in the air,
A rusty sign said 'Park Hill',
But otherwise it was bare.

There were weeds penetrating the platform,
And thistles here and there,

The room where folk once waited in the warm,
Was now beyond repair.

A layer of dust covered the bench,
Stuffing dangled out of a tear,
The atmosphere was a mouldy stench,
And the skirting, a spider's lair.

The building itself was derelict,
Which gave a sense of despair,
Mildew and moss were in conflict,
Ivy hung off the wall like hair.

PATRICK HUMPHRIS

Talking and writing

1 a) Close your eyes. Try to picture the old station which Patrick describes. Which details stick out in your mind?

b) Open your eyes and make a list of the details of the station as you pictured it.

c) Join up with a partner. Discuss your lists and compare the pictures of the old station you created with the picture of it which Patrick presented in the poem. Which details of your pictures were actually described in the poem? Which details did your imaginations add, because they were suggested to you by the poem, though not actually described in it?

2 In a single sentence, sum up the impression of the station buildings and the atmosphere of the station that Patrick is trying to convey in his poem.

3 Take each verse in turn and discuss which details of the old station are included in that verse and the words and phrases that Patrick uses to describe them. Which verse do you think most successfully conveys the impression of the station that Patrick wants to communicate?

4 Try it for yourself. Write a snapshot poem about a room or a building such as:
  a café at closing time
  a classroom before school starts
  a garden shed
  a deserted factory
  a dentist's waiting room
  a ruin
  a warehouse
  a multi-storey car park.
Before you begin, close your eyes and try to visualise the room or building as clearly as you can. Ask yourself questions about all its features such as: what is the floor like? where is the door? how high is the ceiling? etc. Make notes on all the details of the room or building.

When you have finished thinking about all the details, decide what impression you want to give of the room or building. Ask yourself: Is it bright and cheerful or dull and depressing? Is it attractive and welcoming or cold and threatening? Choose two words to sum up the impression of the room or building that you want the poem to give.

When you have decided what impression you want your poem to give, draft it and write it. Show your final draft to your partner. Ask your partner to tell you what impression your poem gives of the room or building and why. Make any alterations you think necessary in view of your partner's comments, then copy it out neatly and, if you want, illustrate it.

The next four poems describe a variety of scenes:

Snapshots: Devon in April

Sheep, dripping like string mops
Are surprised by the sudden sun.

Tear-stained teashop windows
Peer from beneath damp thatches.

Cows, massive as rugby players
Paddle in muddy farmyards.

A smudged rainbow arcs
Over a whitewashed farmhouse.

The skies darken once again.
Soon, terracotta lanes flow.

NIGEL COX

Talking and writing

1 Notice how Nigel Cox uses a sequence of five snapshots in order to present a picture of Devon in April. Talk about how the snapshots link together to convey the impression of how damp and showery it is.

2 Use a similar method in a poem of your own to build up a picture of one of the following:
  town-centre — the week before Christmas
  the beach in August
  school in mid-January
  the woods in November
  the ring-road during the rush-hour.

Almost Still Life

The sun-bleached table
Throws a heavy shadow
In the afternoon light.

A book lies face up,
Beneath it another,
Open and dense with notes.

In a crystal jug
Three wasps float
In an ocean of wine.

Wind lifts
An open page.
The wasps slowly revolve.

NIGEL COX

Talking and writing

1 Why is the poem called 'Almost still life'?

2 Try it yourself. Write a snapshot poem describing a still life scene. For example, you could write about the objects on a workbench, a kitchen table, a dining-room table, a dressing-table or a desk. Or you could write about the objects in a display case in a museum or in a shop, or on a display stand in an exhibition or in a shop window.

3 Alternatively, focus more narrowly and write a still life snapshot poem about something such as a bowl of fruit, a pile of washing, a stack of crockery, a box of toys or a pile of shopping in a supermarket trolley.

4 Try to capture in a snapshot poem a tranquil indoor scene such as:
   someone playing the piano
   a dog or a cat asleep before the fire
   a woman sewing or knitting
   someone sitting in a chair reading
   a baby asleep in its pram or cot.

POETRY 2

View from the Window

Rain washed
Spread of green
Fills the glass.

Ragged hill
Bisecting
Clouds and grass.

Bleached sky
Filigree
Web of trees.

Fingerprints
Diffused
Rings of dust.

The cut hedge
Layered
Like strata.

Butterfly
Lands like a
Signature.

NIGEL COX

Writing

1 Try it yourself. Think of the view from your bedroom window, from the classroom window, from the kitchen window or the living-room window. Select a few details of the scene because a) they stand out, b) they manage to convey what the view is like.

Focus on each of the details in turn. Try to make a comparison in a few words or to find a short phrase to describe each one, in the way that Nigel Cox describes each feature in his poem. Finally, draw a window frame and fit your poem inside it.

2 Write a snapshot poem describing a view from: the top of a tower; a viaduct or bridge; the top of a double-decker bus; the window of a railway carriage; a car on a motorway; an aeroplane; the bridge of a ship; a spacecraft; the summit of a mountain.

Here are two poems with the same pattern:

Sunday Morning

Sunday morning
        and the sun
        bawls
        with
        his big mouth
Yachts
        paper triangles
        of white and blue
        crowd the sloping bay

appearing motionless
as if stuck there
by some infant thumb

beneath a shouting sky

upon a painted sea

WES MAGEE

December Day

December day
        the ground
        brittle with frost
        crunches
        beneath your feet
Trees
        shorn of their leaves
        shiver
        in the thin wind
        thrusting their branches
        defiantly
        skywards

        while their roots dig deeper

        seeking succour in the soil

JOHN FOSTER

Talking and writing

1 Which of the two poems do you prefer? Give your reasons.

2 Write a poem of your own using the same pattern.
For example, you could write about a Friday afternoon or a Monday morning, Christmas Eve or New Year's Day, a November evening or a spring day. Or you could choose a title of your own.

The art of writing a snapshot poem about a scene lies in choosing those details which will create the impression of the scene which you wish to convey. The same applies when you want to write a poem about a person. Here's what the Poet Laureate, Ted Hughes, had to say on the subject in a radio talk:

> The art of choosing just those details about a person which catch his or her life, is not an easy one. You can't make a person come alive in your words simply by describing what he looks like in general, saying, for instance, 'He had a big nose and was bald, and wore blue mostly, but sometimes brown. I think he had brown eyes.' All that tells you nothing: the person described might be a million different people. He might be thin and dwarfish, or immensely fat, and tall. His big nose might be a Roman nose, a spindly knobbly nose, or a hammered-out boxer's nose. From that description, you can't be sure. Your imagination isn't given any definite clue, and so it doesn't go into action, and the whole art of writing is to make your reader's imagination go into action.
>   On the other hand, you don't make things any better

when you try to fit the picture grain by grain into the reader's imagination, as if you were trying to paint it there carefully, as in:

'His brow, at the height of his eyebrows, was precisely seven and a quarter inches across, and from the lowest root of the hair at the mid-point of the hairline along the upper brow to the slight horizontal wrinkle in the saddle of his nose, measured three inches exact. His hair was the colour of rough coconut, parted on the left, closely cropped over the ears and up the back, but perfectly straight, and with no single hair, on any part of his head, more than two and two-third inches long...'

And so on. To describe a man at that rate you'd need a whole book, and you'd be bored reading the first paragraph. But did anything in what I've just read strike my imagination? Yes, one thing did....

Talking

1 What is the one thing which struck Ted Hughes's imagination? Talk about what he says you must try to do if you want to bring a description of a person to life.

2 Here is a prizewinning poem, which Emma Payne wrote when she was sixteen. As you read it, consider and then discuss these questions:
    a) What impression of the boxer is she trying to give?
    b) How do the details she has selected to include in her description each help to convey that impression?
    c) Which of the similes she uses do you find most effective? Say why.

The Boxer

The great iron figure crouches,
Scabs like flowers on his knees,
And his chest is like a mountain
And his legs are thick as trees.

He spits blood like a cherub
In a fountain spouting foam,
Ringed around by swinging ropes
And punters going home.

Broken-knuckled, shiny-eyed,
Battered, bruised, and wet
With droplets like cold rubies,
And laced with bitter sweat.

He crouches in a corner
In his pool of sparkling red
And dreads the jeers which soon will fall
Like blows upon his head.

EMMA PAYNE

Writing

Try it yourself. Write a snapshot poem about a person. It could be about a significant moment in the life of another sportsperson, such as a tennis player or a footballer, a runner or a wrestler. Or it could be about a prisoner or a soldier, a tramp or a pop star, a victim or an outsider, or any person you choose. As you draft your poem, think about what Ted Hughes has to say about how to make a person come alive in your writing.

Finally, here is a snapshot poem about something seen in a poet's imagination:

Snapshot

From my winter window
I mind's-eye see
That shuffling bent old man
So quickly to be me.

JOHN KITCHING

Writing

Try it yourself. Write a snapshot poem about something you see in your imagination. Here is the start of such a poem:

At night-time, when I close my eyes
I mind's-eye see...

9: Letter Poems

The poems in this section are written in the form of letters. The first poem, by Mick Gowar, is a series of Christmas thank-you letters.

Christmas Thank-You's

Dear Auntie
Oh, what a nice jumper
I've always adored powder blue
and fancy you thinking of
orange and pink
for the stripes
how clever of you!

Dear Uncle
The soap is
terrific
So
useful
and such a kind thought and
how did you guess that
I'd just used the last of
the soap that last Christmas brought.

Dear Gran
Many thanks for the hankies
Now I really can't wait for the flu
and the daisies embroidered

in red round the "M"
for Michael
how
thoughtful of you!

Dear Cousin
What socks!
and the same sort you wear
so you must be
the last word in style
and I'm certain you're right that the
luminous green
will make me stand out a mile

Dear Sister
I quite understand your concern
it's a risk sending jam in the post
But I think I've pulled out
all the big bits
of glass
so it won't taste too sharp
spread on toast

Dear Grandad
Don't fret
I'm delighted
So *don't* think your gift will
offend
I'm not at all hurt
that you gave up this year
and just sent me
a fiver
to spend.

MICK GOWAR

Talking and writing

1 What were you thinking of as you read this poem? Did it remind you of any particular birthday or Christmas presents that relatives have given you, which you didn't really want? Has a relative or a family friend ever got muddled up about your age and given you a totally inappropriate present, which would have been more suitable for a younger or older child? Tell each other about disappointing presents you have received at Christmas and for your birthday. What is the most useless present you have ever had?

2 In all but the final letter Mick Gowar has, of course, got his tongue firmly in his cheek. Go through the first five letters and talk about the words and phrases he uses in each one to let the reader know that he is not very excited by that particular present.

3 In the final verse how does he convey to his grandad how pleased he is with his grandad's present?

4 Work in a group of six and prepare a presentation of the poem with each of you reading one of the letters.

5 Try it yourself. Either remember or imagine receiving a particularly awful or disappointing present for Christmas or your birthday. Write a thank-you letter poem in the same style as Mick Gowar.

6 Imagine a relative you do not particularly like has invited you to stay for the weekend at Easter. Write a thank-you letter poem refusing the invitation and making an excuse for not going. Make the excuse as elaborate and imaginative as you like.

A letter of apology

Dear Sir

Dear Sir, I'm sorry about my misbehaviour,
So that's why I'm writing this letter,
I'm sorry about your broken leg,
I hope it's getting better.

I'm sorry about the poison ivy,
I'm sorry about the snake,
I'm sorry I didn't realize,
That your life was at stake.

I'm sorry about the itching powder,
That I put down your back,
I honestly didn't mean,
To get you the sack.

I'm sorry about the curry powder,
That I put in your tea,
I'm sorry about the pin on your seat,
I'm glad you didn't see me.

I'm sorry I made you break your table,
I know you went crazy when you got the bill,
I actually didn't mean... (I'm sorry),
To make you very ill.

I'm sorry about the bar of soap,
That I set outside the door,
The jokes have gone a little too far,
I promise there won't be any more.

So ends this letter of apology
I hope you will accept,
I always thought you were a clever guy,
Who would have looked before you leapt!

STEPHEN DOW

Talking and writing

1 This poem was written by Stephen Dow from Belfast, Northern Ireland at the age of 11. Notice how Stephen has given his poem a clear structure, using four-line verses each of which — apart from the first and last verses — begins with the words 'I'm sorry'. Notice too that the poem has a regular rhyme scheme, with the second and fourth lines of each verse ending in words that rhyme. Sticking to a rhyme scheme when you are writing a poem often poses all sorts of problems. It is usually not too difficult to think of pairs of words that rhyme. The problem is any rhyming words you use must fit in with the sense of the rest of the poem and must not distort the poem's meaning.

Talk about the rhymes Stephen uses. In which verses do you

think the rhymes are most successful? In which verse do you think the rhyme is least successful?

2 Notice that although the poem has a regular rhyme scheme, it does not have a regular rhythm. Work in pairs and go through the poem reading each verse out loud so that you can hear its rhythm. Which verses have the smoothest rhythms?

Do you think it matters that the poem has no regular rhythm? In your opinion, would the poem have been more effective if it had a regular rhythm?

3 Try writing a letter-of-apology poem. Either develop an idea of your own or use one of these ideas:
A letter to your mum apologising for all the things you haven't done but should have done *or* apologising for all the things you do, but she wishes you wouldn't do.
A letter to a neighbour apologising for all the damage your dog did to his garden when it broke through the fence and chased a cat *or* apologising for breaking his window for the third time in a month *or* apologising for riding your bike on the pavement and knocking him over when he was on his way home with two shopping bags full of groceries.
A letter to your teacher apologising for a long list of things you have done wrong, e.g. being late, losing your books, forgetting your PE kit. Here is the start of such a poem:
    Dear Mr McCarthy, I'm writing to say
    How sorry I am for what happened today...
As you draft your poem, think carefully about its rhythm and experiment with using a verse form, such as Stephen's, which has a rhyme scheme. However, remember that meaning matters more than rhyming. If you find it too difficult to think of rhymes that will fit in with the sense of the poem either ask someone to help you or stop trying to make it rhyme and redraft it without a regular rhyme scheme.

A letter of protest

There is nothing so annoying as going to the theatre or cinema and sitting near someone who gives a running commentary on the plot.

At the Theatre

To the lady behind me

Dear Madam, you have seen this play;
I never saw it till today.
You know the details of the plot,
But, let me tell you, I do not.
The author seeks to keep from me
The murderer's identity
And you are not a friend of his
If you keep shouting who it is.
The actors in their funny way
Have several funny things to say,
But they do not amuse me more
If you have said them just before.
The merit of the drama lies,
I understand, in some surprise;

But the surprise must now be small
Since you have just foretold it all.
The lady you have brought with you
Is, I infer, a half-wit too,
But I can understand the piece
Without assistance from your niece.
In short, foul woman, it would suit
Me just as well if you were mute;
In fact, to make my meaning plain,
I trust you will not speak again.
And — may I add one human touch? —
Don't breathe upon my neck so much.

A.P. HERBERT

Writing

Try it yourself. Either develop an idea of your own or write a poem in the form of a letter:
- to the person at the front of the bus who is talking in such a loud voice about all their aches and pains that everyone on the bus can't help but hear;
- to a person sitting opposite you on a train who keeps on and on trying to start a conversation with you, even though it is obvious you want to read your book;
- to a neighbour whose dog wakes you up every morning with its barking and yapping;
- to a younger brother or sister who goes on and on pleading with you to play with him or her, when you have made it quite plain you don't intend to play;
- to someone who insists on tunelessly singing all the words of a song, when you are trying to listen to a record.

Holiday letters and postcards

Wish You Were Here

> Midbay-on-Sea.
> August 9.

Dear Kevin,
        Thought I'd drop a line
With kind regards to everyone.
Wish you were here to share the fun.
Arrived in rain last Saturday,
And will it stop? No blooming way —
Looks like going on for weeks.
Our caravan has fifteen leaks:
It's saturated all our gear.
Kevin, love, wish you were here.
Dad wishes that he hadn't come,
Yesterday he hurt his thumb:
Trapped it in a folding chair —
You should have heard him curse and swear!
He says the beer down here's no good.
The beach has got no sand — just mud;
And what's between us and the sea?
You'll never guess — a cemet'ry;
When I'm out walking with the pup
I go that way — it cheers me up.
My new swimsuit gave Mum a fit:
She says there's not enough of it.
Closing now, Kev, I'm off to bed,
Think I've got flu, I feel half-dead.
Hoping from this exciting whirl,

You're not out with some other girl.
Much love from Misery-on-Sea,
Wish you were here,
Your girl friend,
G.

A postcard poem

We took a trip around the bay.
We came back rather thinner.
We left behind the waves and spray
And also most of dinner!

MAX FATCHEN

Talking and writing

1 Tell each other about some of the most eventful things that have happened to you when you have been either on holiday or on a day out. What is the most disastrous holiday or day out that you have ever had? Make a list of all the things that went wrong.

2 Work with a partner. Imagine the two of you went on a camping holiday that turned out to be full of incident. Write down a list of all the things that could go wrong on such a holiday.

3 Write a 'Wish you were here' letter poem or a postcard poem. If you are stuck for ideas, look through the lists you have just made, to see if there is an idea there which will help you to get started.

10: Haiku, Tanka, Cinquains and Diamond Poems

Haiku

This is a traditional Japanese verse-form. It consists of three lines, which together add up to seventeen syllables. The first line contains five syllables, the second line has seven syllables and the third line has five syllables.

A haiku can be described as a short snapshot poem, which captures a particular moment or feeling. Here are some examples:

Clenched fists of grim clouds,
tense knuckles whitened, waiting
for the first forked flash.

JAMES KIRKUP

Music through thin walls;
Waterfalling guitar notes
Bring fog and autumn leaves.

JOHN KITCHING

Bruised plum sunset sky,
Wind and bitter white-horsed sea,
Solitary star.

JOHN KITCHING

Frosted vapour trail.
White furry caterpillar
looping the sky's leaf.

GEOFFREY HOLLOWAY

Snails, spooled under leaves:
tiny tape-measures dreaming
succulent inches.

GEOFFREY HOLLOWAY

Writing

Try it yourself. Write some haiku. Remember you have only seventeen syllables, so you will have to choose your words very carefully. Take as a starting point either an idea or a picture. Here are some suggestions:

Ideas   *Pictures*

silence   fear   torchbeam   fireworks
waiting   success   horses   swans
daydreams friendship gymnast   rocks
birthdays growing   foxgloves   cranes

Before you begin, here is some advice about writing haiku from the poet David McCord. As you write your haiku, bear it in mind!

'Syllable writing,
Counting out your seventeen,
Doesn't produce poem.

Good haiku need thought:
One simple statement followed
By poet's comment.

The town dump is white
With seagulls, like butterflies
Over a garden.'

DAVID MCCORD

Tanka

This is another traditional Japanese verse-form. It consists of five lines which together add up to 31 syllables. The syllables are arranged in the following way: 5−7−5−7−7. Here are some examples:

Giraffe

The giraffe, gawky
as a pylon, savouring
its flanked tree-shadow:
netted damascene of skin
like sunlight underwater.

GEOFFREY HOLLOWAY

With the Dog

Flip, I feign a throw.
Brink-skidded, he sees my game;
its splashed, ripe redress.
Smash and grab among jewels;
dripping, snout and stick return.

GEOFFREY HOLLOWAY

Reflection

Outside the window
a strange face is looking in
with a funny smile.
—I wonder who it could be?
Oh, good grief, it's only me!

JAMES KIRKUP

Talking and writing

Work in groups and each write one or two tanka on a particular theme. Either choose your own subject or write about one of the following: the city, weathers, the beach, the zoo, the forest, the airport.

Before you start to write, collect ideas by a) doing a brainstorm, b) looking through some old magazines and colour supplements and cutting out pictures. Then, draft your tanka. When you have finished, copy out your poems neatly and mount the pictures and your poems on card to produce a poetry poster.

Cinquains

The cinquain is another five-line verse form. It was invented by an American poet called Adelaide Crapsey. It is shorter than the tanka and consists of only 22 syllables, arranged in the following way: 2−4−6−8−2. Here is a sequence of five cinquains:

The River Cinquains

Dawn
Daybreak:
Between grey rocks,
Silently it wells up
With the force of blood from a wound:
Water.

Morning
Moorland:
Purple heather.
Early sun lights the stream:
Rushing, chattering, swift with fish,
Sparkling.

Afternoon
Townscape:
Water reflects
Grey brickwork, dull windows.
Fishermen stare. The river moves
Slowly.

Evening
Salt-marsh:
Under lead skies
The water slides away.
From the damp banks of sand a few
Birds call.

Night
Moon shines
On open sea:
The swell gleams with silver
And on a distant shore the first
Waves break.

NIGEL COX

Talking and writing

1 Talk about how each verse presents a picture. Pick out the verse which you think presents the most vivid picture. Which words most help to convey that picture?

2 Notice how many of the lines 'run on', i.e. they do not end with a full stop. Instead, the line ends with a comma or no punctuation mark at all, because the sentence is continued on the next line. This helps to give the poem a smoother rhythm than it would otherwise have, if each line ended with a full stop. This is something worth remembering when you try to write your own cinquains.

3 Because the final line of a cinquain consists of only two syllables, it needs to have some impact. Which final line of Nigel Cox's cinquains do you think has the most impact?

4 Either: Write a sequence of cinquains of your own.
You could write about: a day at school, a sporting event (e.g. a tennis match, a football match), a bus or train journey, the seasons, fishing.
Or: Write a cinquain on a particular person, animal or object e.g. a soldier or a conjuror, a goldfish or a kangaroo, a paperweight or a statue.

Diamond poems

Another type of syllable poem is the diamond poem. Here are two examples. In each case, the syllable pattern is: 1–2–3–4–5–4–3–2–1.

    Hawk,
   Eyes bright,
  Scans the moor
  For signs of prey.
 Pinpoints a target.
  Suddenly swoops,
   Claws ready:
    Airborne
     Death.

    Spark
   Glows red
  In wind's breath.
 Struggles for life.
Flickers. Dies. Flickers.
 Bursts into flame.
  Twists and leaps.
   Dancing
    Fire.

Writing

Write your own diamond poem. The rules are simple. In the first half of the poem, add a syllable to each succeeding line; in the second half of the poem take away a syllable from each succeeding line. The size of the diamond depends on the number of syllables you choose to have in the central line of the poem.

 Suitable subjects for diamond poems are ones in which an action of some kind takes place, e.g. catching a fish, snaring a rabbit, a race, a gunshot, an explosion, a collision, breaking a bone, diving into a pool, a space-launch, playing a snooker shot.

11: Adverb Poems

The dictionary definition of an adverb is: any word which adds to the meaning of a verb, adjective or other adverb by telling *how*, *why*, *when* or *where* an action takes place.

VERBS tell of something being done;
To *read*, *count*, *sing*, *laugh*, *jump* or *run*.
How things are done the ADVERBS tell;
As *slowly*, *quickly*, *ill* or *well*.

ANON.

THE ADVERB GAME
Clear a space so that the whole class can sit in a circle. Then, choose one person to go outside the room and ask her/him to count to 100 slowly. While the person is outside the room, the rest of the class chooses an adverb. When the person comes back into the room, she/he has to guess what the adverb is.

Give clues. Get the person who is guessing to ask the different members of the class to perform actions demonstrating what the adverb is. For example, imagine that as a class you have chosen the word 'quietly'. The guesser comes back in and

asks someone to open the window or scratch their ear. The demonstrator performs the action, all the time trying to act quietly. After each demonstration, let the guesser have two guesses.
Note: When you are acting out the adverb, you should not be trying to trick the guesser. Your aim is to communicate what the adverb is by performing your actions 'in the spirit of the adverb'.

Choosing and using adverbs

In the adverb game, did you notice how many of the adverbs you chose ended in -ly? That's because many of the adverbs we use are formed by adding the suffix -ly to a word which is an adjective.

In the next section there is a list of adverbs ending in -ly. They are all adverbs of manner, i.e. they are words we can use to describe the manner in which an action is performed.

Talking and writing

1 Pick out five words from the list which you do not know and look up their meanings in a dictionary.

2 Some of the words in the list have very similar meanings, e.g. rapidly and swiftly. See how many matching pairs of adverbs you can find.

3 Write ten sentences, each of which includes an adverb describing the manner in which an action is performed by a person or an animal. Try to include a reason to explain why the person or animal behaved in that manner. You can make the reason as ridiculous as you like, e.g. The leopard paced anxiously up and down the platform, because the train was late. The witch scowled grimly when she found a puncture in her broomstick.

tightly   calmly   apprehensively   meticulously   warily

angrily   firmly   sadly   idly   suspiciously   jauntily   furtively

awkwardly   cunningly   cautiously   furiously   relentlessly

dejectedly   swiftly   morosely   shiftily   gracefully   anxiously

carefully   slyly   guiltily   deftly   rapidly   nervously   nimbly

nonchalantly   stealthily   ·craftily   placidly   grimly

wickedly   cruelly   eagerly   daintily   clumsily   gently

frantically   jocularly   sternly   jovially   viciously   meanly

sharply   restlessly   menacingly   urgently   maliciously

valiantly   fiercely   boldly   joyfully   monstrously

desperately

Note: In the examples in question 3 the adverb has been placed immediately after the verb it qualifies. But it does not *have* to be placed there. You can put the adverb in several different places in a sentence; it all depends on how much emphasis you want to put on the adverb, e.g.

Anxiously the leopard paced up and down the platform...
The leopard paced anxiously up and down the platform...
The leopard paced up and down the platform anxiously...

In the sentences you write, experiment with placing the adverb in different places.

4 Here are two stories for you to complete, using adverbs to fill in the gaps:

The message
The telephone rang.....
The woman picked up the receiver.....
She listened.....
She put down the receiver.....
Tears started to roll down her cheeks.....

The escape
The prisoner waited.....
The cell-door was pushed open.....
Her friend whispered.....
She picked up the bundle.....
They set off down the corridor.....

5 See if you can write a similar five-line story in which each sentence ends with an adverb. Write a story about either an accident or a haunting or make up a title of your own.

Adverb poems

Slowly

Slowly the tide creeps up the sand,
Slowly the shadows cross the land.
Slowly the cart-horse pulls his mile,
Slowly the old man mounts the stile.

Slowly the hands move round the clock,
Slowly the dew dries on the dock.
Slow is the snail — but slowest of all
The green moss spreads on the old brick wall.

JAMES REEVES

Writing

Write a similar poem. Either choose an adverb yourself or use one from this list: quietly, gently, softly, lightly, swiftly, brightly, loudly.

Before you begin, collect your ideas together by drawing a spidergram. A spidergram is a diagram in the shape of a spider. Draw an oval shape for the spider's body and write the name of your topic in it. Then, draw lines to represent the spider's legs. As you think of an idea write it down by one of the lines.

Below is the start of a spidergram for the word 'rapidly'. Suggest other ideas to complete the diagram, then draw a spidergram of your own for the word you have chosen.

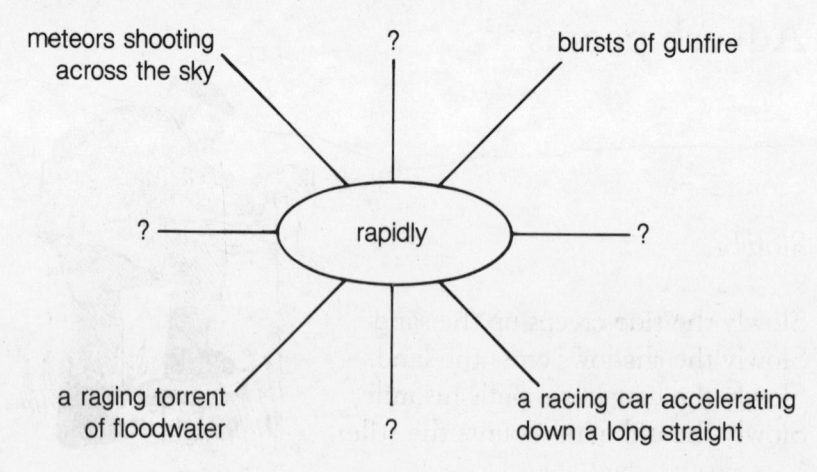

- meteors shooting across the sky
- ?
- bursts of gunfire
- ?
- rapidly
- ?
- a raging torrent of floodwater
- ?
- a racing car accelerating down a long straight

accidentally

accidentally
broke a teacup —
reminds me
how good it feels
to break things

ISHIKAWA TAKUBOKU

Writing

1 Try it yourself. Complete one of these poems which follow the same pattern:

suddenly	*suddenly*	*suddenly*
suddenly	suddenly	suddenly
saw a....	heard a....	touched a....
reminds me	reminds me	reminds me
....	....	....
....	....	....

Note: There is no need to stick rigidly to the pattern. If you want, a) use more than one word to complete line two; b) start line four with 'of' rather than 'how'; c) use more than four words in lines four and five.

Here is one attempt at such a poem:

Suddenly

suddenly
felt a hand gripping my wrist
reminds me
how a prisoner must feel
as the handcuffs are snapped on.

2 Write an adverb poem of your own using a similar pattern. Either choose an adverb yourself or use one of the following: anxiously, finally, cautiously, accidentally.

How happily she laughs!

How happily she
   laughs! on and on and on, a
     waterfall of sound.

IAN SERRAILLIER

Writing

Write a similar type of comparison poem. Start your poem, as Ian Serraillier does, with a statement describing how something is done by using an adverb. Either choose your own opening or use one of these openings:

| How beautifully she... | How deftly she... |
| How slyly the... | How gracefully she... |

Note: Ian Serraillier's poem is in the form of a haiku (see page 97). If you want, you could try to shape your poem as a haiku. Alternatively, you could write a two-line comparison poem, like this one:

> How wickedly the wolf grins:
> its bared teeth, two rows of unsheathed daggers.

London Snow

When men were all asleep the snow came flying,
In large white flakes falling on the city brown,
Stealthily and perpetually settling and loosely lying,
Hushing the latest traffic of the drowsy town;
Deadening, muffling, stifling its murmurs failing;
Lazily and incessantly floating down and down;
Silently sifting and veiling road, roof and railing
Hiding difference, making unevenness even,
Into angles and crevices softly drifting and sailing.

from *London Snow* by ROBERT BRIDGES

Talking and writing

1 Talk about the words Robert Bridges uses to describe how the snow falls.

2 Pick out the line which enables you to picture most clearly the snow falling on the sleeping town. Say why.

3 The poem describes a scene in which there is a lot of movement. So, not surprisingly, it is full of verbs and adverbs. Write a poem on one of the following: a windy night, a sudden shower, a storm at sea, a blizzard or a gale. Think carefully about the verbs and adverbs you choose to try to convey a picture of the scene you are describing.

Finally, here is an adverb poem to read aloud. Work with a partner and together prepare a presentation of Philip C. Gross's poem In the Rush-hour Traffic Jam.

In the Rush-hour Traffic Jam

Wearily, drearily, stiff with strain
I stared through the windows streaked with rain
At the truck to the front and the bus to the rear,
Fearing the traffic just never would clear.

Moodily, broodily turning my gaze
Away from the stifling blue exhaust haze,
Grumbling as miserably, creeping like snails,
Commuters inched homeward, noses to tails.

Strangely, amazingly there to the right
I noticed the most incongruous sight
Of an elderly gentleman, relaxed at the wheel,
The warmth of whose smile I could virtually feel.

Unhappily, snappily, ill-mannered lout,
I said 'What are you so happy about?'
'Son', he said gently, 'try being like me
'When you find that you're somewhere you don't want to be.

'Gently, intently I empty my mind
And over displeasure I draw down a blind
Frustration flows out, mem'ries flood in
And I'm back to my boyhood away from the din.

Lazily, daisily in meadow I lie,
Exploring cloud mountains in Summer's blue sky,
Warmed by the sun and cooled by the breeze,
Lulled by the birdsong filling the trees.

Slowly, silently parting the sedge,
That's growing down to the water's edge,
I see shadowy fish in sparkling rill.
That's where memories take me still.'

Beguilingly, smilingly with twinkling eye,
He waved a hand in brief goodbye,
Leaving me lost in remembered dreams
Of Summers and sunshine, meadows and streams.

PHILIP C. GROSS

12: Story Poems

When you write a story poem, one decision you have to make is whether to write your poem in the first person (I) or in the third person (he, she or it).

First-person story poems

The hurricane

I can remember seeing
the little ravine like a big river.
Houses blown away.
The roof of my grandmother's house
blown away.
Mango branches, branches of trees.

I can remember seeing
my uncle carrying my cousin.
She had very bad legs
and she could not walk.

I can remember my mother
with my sister on her shoulder.
She looked so poorly
my mother thought she was dead.
People told her
to throw the dead child away.
But my mother said,
'No, I will bury her after the hurricane.'

I can remember we kept going
and when we reached the next house
we stopped there.

And soon after the hurricane was over.

YVONNE ROBERTS

Writing

Notice how in this story poem Yvonne Roberts uses the technique of repeating the same introductory phrase at the start of each section. Write a first-person story poem either about a dramatic incident in your own life or in which you imagine yourself involved in a dramatic incident such as a bomb scare, a fire, a rescue or a crash. Develop your poem in sections. Here are some introductory phrases you could use to start each section:
   I'll never forget...
   I can still (see/hear/picture/feel...)
   That morning/afternoon/evening...
   When I think back...

Third-person story poems

Here are two third-person story poems:

Don' Go Ova Dere

Barry madda tell im
But Barry wouldn't hear,
Barry fada warn im
But Barry didn' care.
'Don' go ova dere, bwoy,
Don' go ova dere.'

Barry sista beg im
Barry pull her hair,
Barry brother bet im
'You can't go ova dere.'
'I can go ova dere, bwoy,
I can go ova dere.'

Barry get a big bag,
Barry climb de gate,
Barry granny call im
But Barry couldn't wait,
Im wan' get ova dere, bwoy,
Before it get too late.

Barry see de plum tree
Im didn' see de bull,
Barry thinkin' bout de plums
'Gwine get dis big bag full'.
De bull get up an' shake, bwoy,
An gi de rope a pull.

De rope slip off de pole
But Barry didn' see,
De bull begin to stretch im foot den
Barry climb de tree.
Barry start fe eat bwoy,
Firs' one, den two, den three.

Barry nearly full de bag
An den im hear a soun'
Barry hol' de plum limb tight
An start fe look aroun'
When im see de bull, bwoy,
Im nearly tumble down.

Night a come, de bull naw move,
From unda de plum tree,
Barry madda wondering
Whey Barry coulda be.
Barry getting tired, bwoy,
Of sittin' in dat tree.

An Barry dis realise
Him neva know before,
Sey de tree did full o' black ants
But now im know fe sure.
For some begin fe bite im, bwoy,
Den more, an more, an more.

De bull lay down fe wait it out,
Barry mek a jump,
De bag o' plum drop out de tree
An Barry hear a thump.
By early de nex' mawnin', bwoy,
Dat bull gwine have a lump.

De plum so frighten dat po' bull
Im start fe run too late,
Im a gallop afta Barry
But Barry jump de gate.
De bull jus' stamp im foot, bwoy,
Im yeye dem full o' hate.

When Barry ketch a im yard,
What a state im in!
Im los' im bag, im clothes mud up,
An mud deh pon im chin.
An whey de black ants bite im
Feba bull-frog skin.

Barry fada spank im,
Im madda sey im sin,
Barry sista scold im
But Barry only grin,
For Barry brother shake im head
An sey, 'Barry, yuh win!'

VALERIE BLOOM

The Cane

    The teacher
had some thin springy sticks
      for making kites.

    Reminds me
of the old days, he said;
      and swished one.

    The children
near his desk laughed nervously,
      and pushed closer.

    A cheeky girl
held out her cheeky hand.
      Go on, Sir!

    said her friends.
Give her the stick, she's always
      playing up.

    The teacher
paused, then did as he was told.
      Just a tap.

    Oh, Sir!
We're going to tell on you,
      The children said.

    Other children
left their seats and crowded round
      the teacher's desk.

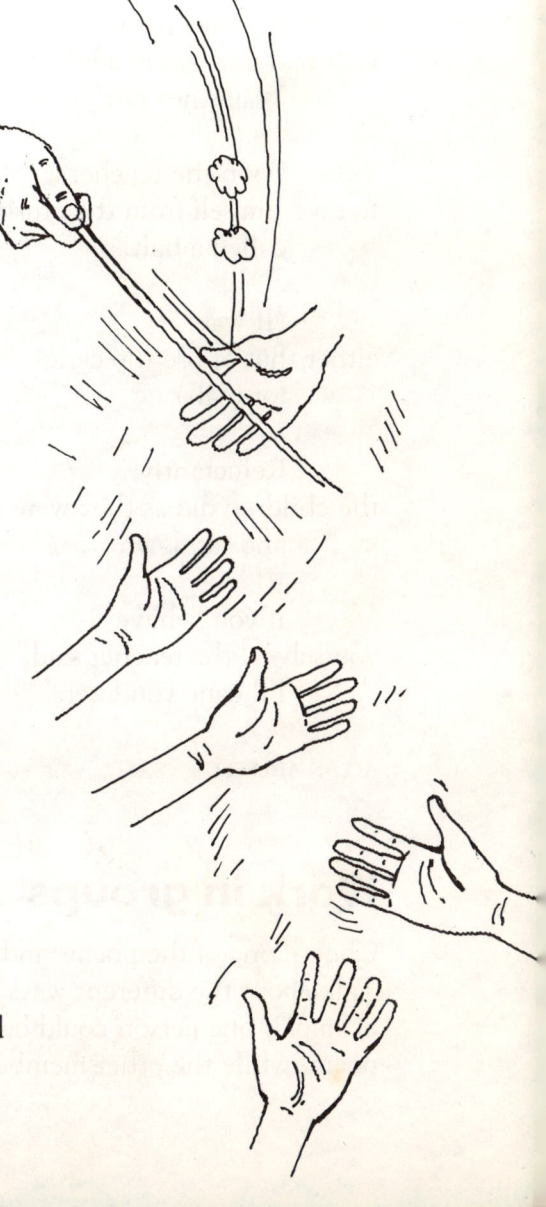

>   Other hands
> went out. Making kites was soon
>   forgotten.
>
>   My turn next!
> He's had one go already!
>   That's not fair!
>
>   Soon the teacher,
> to save himself from the crush
>   called a halt.
>
>   (It was
> either that or use the cane
>   for real.)
>
>   Reluctantly,
> the children did as they were told
>   and sat down.
>
>   If you behave
> yourselves, the teacher said,
>   I'll cane you later.

ALLAN AHLBERG

Work in groups

Choose one of the poems and prepare a presentation of it. Talk about the different ways you could present it. For example, one person could be a narrator, reading the whole poem, while the other members of the group act it out.

Alternatively, you could divide the poem up so that each member of the group speaks certain lines. Whatever you decide to do, consider whether using music and sound effects would be a good idea. Practise your presentations, then in turn show them to the rest of the class. Then, discuss whose presentation worked best and why.

Writing

Write a third-person story poem about an incident involving a girl or a boy, like Barry, or about an incident that occurred in class one day. Develop your poem so that it has a pattern of verses, in the same way that both Valerie Bloom's and Allan Ahlberg's poems have a pattern. If you use a pattern similar to Valerie Bloom's and decide to try to make your poem rhyme, then work hard as you draft your poem to make sure that the rhymes always fit in with the sense of the poem.

Limericks

One of the most popular forms of story poem is the five-line nonsense verse, known as the limerick. It was made famous by the nineteenth-century poet Edward Lear. Here are some examples:

There was a young fellow named Mark
Who would swim out to sea in the dark;
   On these nocturnal trips
   He observed several ships...
Until he was observed. By a shark.

There was an old man who averred
He had learned how to fly like a bird.
    Cheered by thousands of people
    He leapt from the steeple—
This tomb states the date it occurred.

There was a young parson named Perkins
Exceedingly fond of small gherkins.
    One summer at tea
    He ate forty-three,
Which pickled his internal workins.

A skeleton once in Khartoum
Invited a ghost to his room;
    They spent the whole night
    In the eeriest fright
As to which should be frightened of whom.

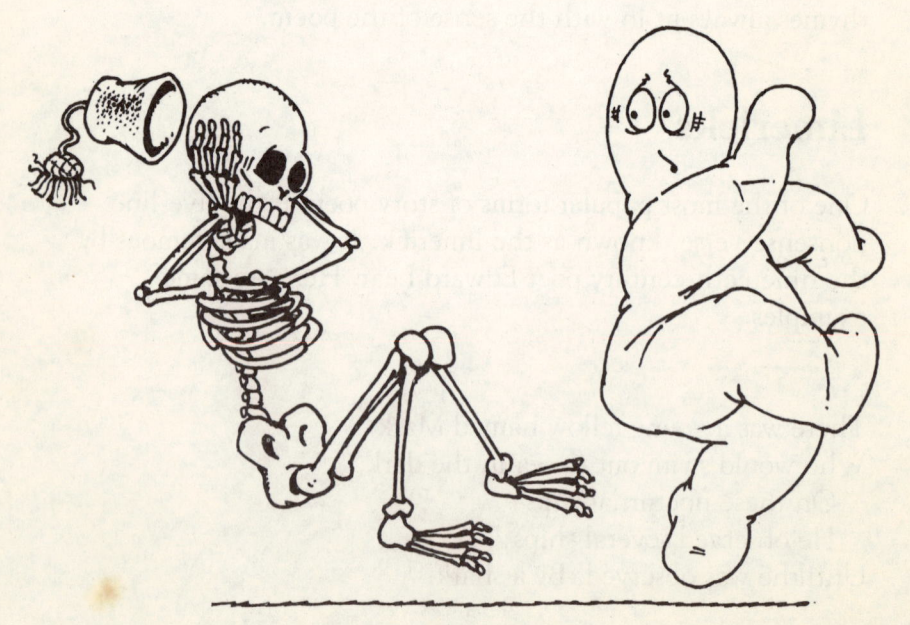

Writing

Notice how each limerick has the same pattern.
- Lines 1, 2 and 5 are the same length and have the same rhythm. They also end with the same rhyme.
- Lines 3 and 4 are short lines, with the same length, rhythm and rhyme.

Try it yourself.

1 Here is a limerick for you to complete:

> There was a young girl from Montrose
> Who had an extremely long nose.
>   She once gave a sneeze
>   (*Short line, rhymes with sneeze*)
> (*A longer line, rhyming with nose*)

Note: Since a limerick is a humorous poem, it needs to have a strong last line, which acts like the punchline of a joke.

2 Now write some complete limericks of your own. Either make up your own first lines or use some of these:

> There once was a teacher called Blains...
> A magician's apprentice called Matt...
> A foolish young student from Bly...
> An eccentric young lady called Gray...
> There once was a farmer called Wright...

Note: The last of these need not be a farmer. It could be anyone with a two-syllable occupation — a postman, a dentist, a doctor, a soldier, etc.

Finally, here is a different kind of story poem:

Murder story

```
moon      cloak       cold
peep      flutter     creep
    hammer    prey
    shadow   hunt
       soft  lone
       girl  walk
eye       fear        blood
ember     stalk       drunk
    black    claw
    leap     death
        deaf
        night
```

ANDREW RAWLINSON

Writing

Write a similar poem. Either make up your own title or use one of the following titles: Ghost Story; Space Visitor; Earthquake; Riot Story; Collision; False Alarm; Mystery Story; The Fight.

Plan your poem by making lists of words. Then, experiment with different words in different positions.

Note: Andrew Rawlinson's poem consists of nouns, verbs and adjectives only. See if you can also include at least one or two adverbs in your poem. (Refer to section 11 on adverbs.)